COST-EFFECTIVE STRATEGIES FOR CLIENT/SERVER SYSTEMS

Bernard H. Boar

AT&T

Global Information Solutions

John Wiley & Sons, Inc.
New York • Chichester • Brisbane • Toronto • Singapore

Copyright © 1996 by AT&T
Published by John Wiley & Sons, Inc.

The opinions expressed in this book are those of the author and do not necessarily represent those of AT&T.

Library of Congress Cataloging-in-Publication Data

ISBN 0-471-12846-5

Printed in the United States of America

10 9 8 7 6 5 4 3 2 1

For Diane, Jessica and Debbie—
With Love Always

Other Books by the Author

Abend Debugging for COBOL Programmers

Application Prototyping: A Requirements Definition Strategy for the 80s

Implementing Client/Server Computing: A Strategic Perspective

The Art of Strategic Planning for Information Technology: Crafting Strategy for the 90s

The Art of Strategic Planning for Information Technology: Crafting Strategy for the 90s (Chinese Edition)

Practical Steps for Aligning Information Technology with Business Strategies: How to Achieve a Competitive Advantage

The opinions expressed in this book are those of the author and do not necessarily represent those of AT&T.

On Strategy

Vision is seeing victory before it exists.
This is the strategist way to strategic triumph.

—Sun Tzu, *The Art of War*

Contents

Foreword

The last four years have been an exceptional period of intense change and excitement in the information technology (I/T) industry. The reach of information technology is accelerating, the range and types of information that can be shared are growing, and, as never before, heterogeneous computing technologies can be combined to create new computing platforms and applications. With all this activity, however, has come tremendous pressure on the I/T organization for results. The business demands better value for their I/T dollars, new technologies must be rapidly integrated into the technology portfolio, and outsourcers, system integrators, and consultants are competing for user attention and business. Never before has corporate I/T leadership been in such urgent need of insightful strategic advice.

Likewise, the last four years have been a unique creative period for Bernie. This book completes his tetralogy on the subjects of information technology strategy and client/server computing. The books provide peerless advice on strategy and tactics for the harried I/T executive. Advice and counsel that is best described as "deep and far reaching."

Though we can recommend with confidence that you will benefit greatly from reading any and all of the books of the tetralogy, we believe that this book is particularly valuable because it can be read and applied at any of three varied levels:

1. It offers direct cogent strategic advice on how to maximize the value of moving to client/server computing. The analysis is unique and thought-provoking.
2. It serves as an example of broad strategic thinking applied to the specific problems of information technology. Whether you agree or disagree with the conclusions, the analytical tech-

niques used and the chain of thought exercised will provide an excellence reference of how strategic I/T problems should be approached.

3. It provides for the application of Sunian strategy to the discipline of information technology. Given the longstanding strategic problems that have constrained the effective use of I/T in the building and sustaining of competitive advantage for the business, the application of Sunian strategy to I/T problems offers a fresh approach to solving these important and persistent challenges.

You may therefore benefit form this book immediately at one level that reflects your immediate formidable tasks and, perhaps, later, in harmony with changed responsibilities, benefit at a completely different level.

AT&T is in the information movement and management business. It sells information technologies to clients world-wide and is, itself, one of the largest consumers of I/T. The thinking contained in this book represents the types of ideas that help us compete in a superior manner in the global marketplace every day. It will help you solve the enduring, universal and real problem of information technology; the need for the I/T assets to be able to change quicker than the business.

Jeanne Nolan, Ph.D.

Jeanne M. Nolan

Managing Partner
Knowledge Transfer Consulting Services
AT&T Global Information Solutions

Preface

This is a book of loosely coupled essays on the subject of client/server computing. The chapters are coupled in that they all focus on the same broad subject, client/server computing, but from distinct perspectives. The chapters are loosely related in that they are all semi-independent essays. Although they each make references to each other to avoid any redundant presentation of ideas and are delivered in a logical progression, each stands alone and makes its own unique arguments. The chapters should be read in numerical order to assure understanding of explicit and implicit references to ideas introduced in prior chapters.

These essays originated as customer seminars from my consulting practice at AT&T. They were developed in response to two related marketplace observations. The first observation was that while client/server computing is vigorously growing and displacing the aging and antiquated monolithic host-centered computing model, users are clearly not accruing all the anticipated benefits. Having made the giant leap forward across the computing paradigm chasm, they are experiencing a variety of disappointments in terms of cost savings, productivity improvements, system flexibility, and so on. The second observation is the birth and growth of a small but vocal, articulate, and influential group of gurus, pundits, oracles, market researchers, vendors, and users who are asserting that client/server computing is not nearly as beneficial as claimed. This eclectic group argues, often quite persuasively but always with zealous righteousness, that client/server computing is revealing itself under fire to be but just another in the seemingly endless procession of over-hyped information technology (I/T) fads. The more radical members of this group argue that the migration to client/server computing should be abated and mainframe hegemony must be reestablished as the mainstay of corporate information technology. To what had rapidly become a "no-brainer" decision, migrating to a client/server architecture, fear, uncertainty and doubt (FUD) is being restored.

My reaction to both these observations, about those who are trying to migrate but are experiencing obstacles and those who resist and leverage the failures of others as anti-client/server evidence, is that they are both rooted in the same problem. Sun Tzu, the father of strategy, said that strategy was to be "deep and far reaching."[1] When it was such, "you could win even before you fight." I believe that the core problem shared by both these groups is their fundamental strategic misunderstanding of client/server computing. The implementers, although well intentioned, are disappointed because their implementations and expectations have not been shaped in a deep and far-reaching manner. The second group, hoping to preserve what has made them successful in the past, have completely failed to grasp the strategic value proposition of client/server computing. There thinking, in Sunian terms, is incredibly "shallow and nearsighted."

These essays, then, are a response to these observations. With a single set of essays, we hope to simultaneously accomplish dual objectives:

1. For those who have or intend to migrate to client/sever, we would like to provide deep and far-reaching counsel so that their implementations will far exceed their expectations. The success of client/server migration is a function of the strategy and tactics deployed. The technology is inanimate. It is your implementation decisions that create success or failure. We will therefore provide a singular analysis of what client/server is and how to implement it so that the implementation will accrue the maximum possible value for the business.

---

[1]The full Sun Tzu quote is as follows:

When your strategy is deep and far reaching, then what you gain by your calculations is much, so you can win before you even fight. When your strategic thinking is shallow and near-sighted, then what you gain by your calculations is little, so you lose before your do battle. Much strategy prevails over little strategy, so those with no strategy cannot help but be defeated. Therefore it is said that victorious warriors win first and then go to war, while defeated warriors go to war first and then seek to win.

2. For those who are opposed to client/server computing (i.e., the current card-carrying membership of the Mainframe Preservation Society [MPS]), we will provide a strategic refutation to their arguments. In this way, they might understand where their logic has failed them and led them astray. We hope they will reconsider their positions so that they might, at best, share in the advantages of client/server computing and, at minimum, stop deterring indecisive information technology decision makers from proceeding with an expeditious client/server implementation.

The first and most important principle is that the strategy must be right. If the strategy is wrong or the problem strategically misunderstood, it is not surprising that the results are less than satisfactory. No amount of charismatic leadership, extraordinary effort, or tactical brilliance will compensate for a fundamentally wrong strategy.

Given the competitive pressures that are facing all companies today, resolving the issue of monolithic host-centered or client/server computing is not a technology problem but a business problem of the utmost urgency. As we are propelled in fast forward toward the next millennium, it is obvious that businesses are being faced with "grand challenges." Markets are no longer content to be segmented; they fracture into fragments of one. Competencies that had assured long-term prosperity are reversed by agile competitors and transformed into liabilities. While we are exhorted to cut costs to the minimum, we are simultaneously implored to add value and differentiate. Viewing the forthcoming years under the rubric of "grand challenges" is most appropriate and accurate.

The answer to business "grand challenges" lies where it has always lain—in the building, sustaining, and compounding of competitive advantage. Regardless of the pressing business chaos swirling about you, if you can build advantages for the customer, the customer will come. Those with more advantages win; those with fewer advantages lose. It really is that elementary.

The object of business strategy, then, is the building, sustaining, and compounding of competitive advantage to win markets (customers). The reason for advantages, however, is competition. It is the existence of able competitors who are aggressively competing for the same prize (the customer) that creates the need for advantage. Without competition, the running of a business is reduced to problem in administration. So the purpose of advantage is to win customers, but the reason for advantage is competition.

Few assets offer the potential to build as robust and varied advantage as does information technology. Businesses may be viewed and understood as massively parallel human and mechanized information-processing entities. How information is collected, moved, processed, analyzed, stored, and accessed is fundamental to business success. Most companies, though they barely realize it, are first and foremost in the information movement and management business. If information movement and management is not their primary business, it certainly is the first adjunct to it.

It is because of the importance of information technology to business success that the issue of client/server computing is so important. If it is as detrimental as the Mainframe Preservation Society would have us believe, then a company moving to it makes a most imprudent and risky decision. If it as beneficial as its supporters claim, failure to migrate in a prompt and orderly manner will leave a business at grave marketplace peril. This is the business background of the mainframe–client/server debate, and this is why understanding client/server strategically is so important. The core questions surrounding the monolithic host-centered computing or client/server debate are not merely technology questions, they are imperative business questions.

This book is structured into nine loosely coupled chapters as follows:

- *Chapter 1: The Mainframe Preservation Society (MPS)*
  This chapter introduces the reader to the primary arguments against client/server computing. The sources for these arguments are articles, brochures, and other media presentations by a wide variety of mainframe advocates in the I/T industry. Unquestionably, the most damaging myth presented is the fiction that client/server computing is more expensive than host-centered computing.
- *Chapter 2: Corporate Strategy, Information Technology and Client/Server Computing*
  This chapter provides answers to two fundamental questions of I/T strategy:

  1. How should the I/T organization be structured to perfectly align with the corporate strategy of a global multibusiness (multiple strategic business unit) corporation?

2. How, if at all, does client/server computing contribute to the business–I/T strategic alignment?

In this way, we commence our analysis with an understanding of how business strategy drives I/T strategy, which in turn dictates the selection of an I/T architecture.

- *Chapter 3: Understanding Client/Server Computing Strategically*
  This chapter provides a strategic response to the Mainframe Preservation Society. Using the strategic frameworks of S curve analysis, value positioning, strategic alignment, strategic paradox, and vision, this chapter explains why the Mainframe Preservation Society arguments are not only fallacious but demonstrate a fundamental absence of strategic analysis and thinking. From this chapter the reader will gain an appreciation of how client/server computing offers a rare and exciting strategic opportunity for the business.
- *Chapter 4: The Economics of Client/Server Computing*
  This chapter provides a refutation of the most outrageous myth asserted by the Mainframe Preservation Society, which is, of course, that client/server computing is at best equal in cost to mainframe computing, is at worst 14.3 times more expensive, and is most likely 3 to 4 times more expensive. The myth is exposed by showing that client/server savings should not be understood in terms of traditional mainframe economies of scale but in terms of economies of sharing. Client/server savings are demonstrated to be a function of architectural discipline, and, to the contrary of the MPS assertions, properly implemented, there is every reason to believe that client/server will offer significant cost benefits over mainframe computing.
- *Chapter 5: Data Architecture, Data Placement, and a Distributed Database in a Client/Server Environment*
  This chapter analyzes the strategic challenge of distributing data across the client/server enterprise. One of the most important architectural design decisions in a client/server architecture is the placement and partitioning of databases across the client/server network. There are innumerable choices as the size of your interoperable client/server environment grows. This chapter develops a decision model of how to make cost-effective database placement and partitioning decisions.

- *Chapter 6: Reenginering the Information Technology Organization for Client/Server Computing*
  This chapter presents an analysis of the strategic reengineering required to reposition the I/T organization from an internal monopoly supplier of monolithic host-centered computing to a competitive supplier of a whole plethora of information technology solutions built around client/server computing. Reengineering issues covered include the internal economy, core competencies, processes, human resource architecture, revised vendor relationships, strategic planning methodologies, I/T architecture, and organizational structure. From this chapter the reader will learn a generic framework that can be applied to any I/T organization to support it in a world-class implementation of client/server computing.
- *Chapter 7:* The Art of War *and Client/Server Computing*
  This chapter will analyze client/server computing from the perspective of *The Art of War,* Sun Tzu's great treatise on strategy, which provides guidelines on how to develop invincible strategy. This chapter will explain how client/server computing offers unique opportunities to realize an *The Art of War* strategy.
- *Chapter 8: The Mainframe Empire Strikes Back*
  This chapter provides answers to common questions I have been asked about the arguments presented in this book. As I have given these seminars around the world, many attendees have questioned the logic of my arguments. This chapter shares that question and answer exchange.
- *Chapter 9: Vision Is Seeing Victory Before It Exists*
  This chapter provides a reprise of the arguments presented. Most important, it emphasizes the primacy of vision to strategic success and how client/server computing can help develop and realize a winning vision for the I/T organization and the business.

By structuring the book in this manner, we accomplish two complementary goals; first we refute the well intentioned but misdirected interpretations of the MPS and, secondarily, we develop the most cost efficient and effective strategies for implementing client/server computing.

This book should be of interest to members of the information technology and business community who are concerned with information technology, business strategy, and planning. Typical readers would have senior management titles (CIO, VP of I/T, VP of Strategy, Director of I/T) or titles that include words such as *planner, architecture, designer, trainer, partner, strategist* or *officer.* The book will most likely not be of interest to technical people who are primarily interested in the bits, bytes, pixels, packets, MIPS, or widgets of computing unless they wish to expand their technology-centric perspective to that of business strategy.

To avoid surprise on your part, let me end the preface by being candid. The arguments contained herein are not "balanced." It is not my intent to make everyone happy and feel good about their current beliefs. While it is superficially nice to offer balanced commentary to soothe the political and emotive needs of a heterogeneous audience, it is in reality much kinder to confront the truth, however unpleasant it may be in the short term, so that corrective and remedial actions may be taken before an organization becomes moribund. However, it is not my intent to offer any offense. Although my arguments may be blunt, my intentions are explanatory. Since some of the writings of the MPS are confrontational, pejorative, full of invective, and combative as opposed to an enlightened debate, my pen sometimes responds in kind. Nevertheless, I request your pardon in advance if I am too pointed and frank in my response and affront you in any manner. My defense of client/server is not apologetic, it is spirited.

It is my intention to strategically analyze the situation as it is in truth so that a viable path to success may be selected. I believe that the arguments of the Mainframe Preservation Society are fallacious. They demonstrate a serious lack of strategic acumen, and following them will lead one to ruin. I also believe that the common arguments for adopting client/server computing, although well-intentioned and correct, are not good enough. If we are to maximize the benefits from the great host-centered to client/server migration, we must offer a compelling strategic logic; a logic of ideas that are "deep and far reaching." I suspect that whether you agree or disagree with my arguments, you will certainly find them most interesting, stimulating, novel, and provocative. At minimum, we will elevate the level of future debate to Sunian standards.

Bernard H. Boar
East Brunswick, New Jersey
May, 1995

Acknowledgments

Though I write alone, I do not learn alone. Many of my ideas are the results of extensive exchanges with clients and colleagues. As there are too many to name individually, I thank you all collectively. I would like to thank the Art department at AT&T Bell Laboratories in Holmdel NJ who provided peerless support in creating the artwork for this book. I would particularly like to thank Professor Levent Orman of Cornell University whose work on I/T architecture provides the basis for Chapter 4. I would also like to thank all those owners of intellectual property who graciously granted permission for me to include their material. Appropriate citations are made at the point of use. Of course, I would like to thank my management team at AT&T Global Information Solutions who provide a fertile environment for developing thought leadership which is essential to the continual health of our industry.

Lastly, I would like to acknowledge the decisive influence of one book, *The Art of War* by Sun Tzu, on my thinking. Appendix D provides a bibliography of translations. All the quotes in this book from *The Art of War* come from that list. If your strategic intent is too become a world class I/T strategist, I cannot urge you too strongly to become a devoted student of *The Art of War*. It contains all one needs to know about strategy. One just needs to discover it.

Acronyms

ACID	Atomicity, Consistency, Isolation, and Durability
API	Application Program Interface
CPU	Central Processing Unit
C/S	Client/Server
CSC	Client/Server Computing
CSCA	Client/Server Computing Architecture
CSMS	Customer Satisfaction Measurement System
CSPLA	The Client/Server Peoples Liberation Army
DBMS	Database Management System
DDB	Distributed Database
DRAM	Dynamic Random Access Memory
DT	Data Layer
DTM	Distributed Transaction Monitor
EDI	Electronic Data Interchange
E-Mail	Electronic Mail
FUD	Fear, Uncertainty, and Doubt
IM&M	Information Movement and Management
IMS	Information Management System
I/O	Input/Output
IPC	Interprocess Communication
ISC	Intersystem Coupling
I/T	Information Technology
JCL	Job-Control Language
LAN	Local Area Network
MIPS	Millions of Instructions per Second
MPS	The Mainframe Preservation Society
MSC	Multiple System Coupling
OLTP	On-line Transaction Processing
OSS	Operations Support System

PC	Personal Computer
PCM	Plug-Compatible Manufacturer
PN	Presentation Software Layer
PR	Processing Software Layer
PSCS	The Proprietary System Conservation Society
SBU	Strategic Business Unit
SQL	Structured Query Language
TPM	Teleprocessing Monitor
WAN	Wide Area Network
4th GL	Fourth Generation Language

1

The Mainframe Preservation Society

As the information technology (I/T) community met the halfway mark of the 1990s, it certainly appeared, to even the most casual observer, that client/server computing had won. DEC, AMDAHL, and FUJITSU were all in decline, and, following a precipitous fall, IBM was going diagonally while the client/server computing companies, Microsoft, Oracle, SYBASE, Cisco, AT&T, and so on were all in steep ascent. Client/server, in all its variations, was *the* subject of the industry press, of almost all new and exciting vendor product announcements, and of countless market research reports, and was the principal or adjunct theme of nearly all industry conferences. The computing future was effortlessly predictable, and it was, with near unanimity, a client/server future. Architecture forecasts, such as those illustrated in Figure 1.1, had become quite mundane. The computing architecture contest was a fait accompli, and client/server was the new architecture champion, dethroning the aging and tiring monolithic host-centered computing model.

The underlying economics of computing's basic technologies was driving the migration. Microprocessor performance trends (Figure 1.2), memory performance trends (Figure 1.3), and storage performance trends (Figure 1.4) all conspired against the mainframe and prompted the gold rush to computing solutions based on the client/server framework. It was extremely rare, if it was possible at all, to find any published price/performance trends that favored host-based computing.

Against this background, the following justifications were typically given as the rationale for migrating from host-based computing to client/server computing:

- *Cost savings:* Client/server solutions would be life cycle cheaper.

1

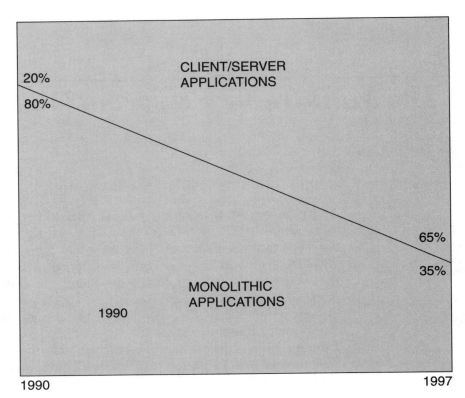

Figure 1.1   Architecture forecast. Typical I/T architecture forecasts show a clear shift to client/server computing from monolithic host-centered computing.

- *Technology accessibility:* All new and attractive technologies would be client/server based.
- *Staff attraction:* To maintain and attract a competent staff, it would be necessary to be current with client/server technology.
- *Development speed:* Client/server application development was much quicker.
- *Productivity:* The use of client/sever would offer dual productivity benefits. The developers would be substantially more productive, and the resulting applications would dramatically increase the productivity of the business users.
- *Reengineering support:* most of the engaging technologies that could be used to reengineer business processes were client/server based.

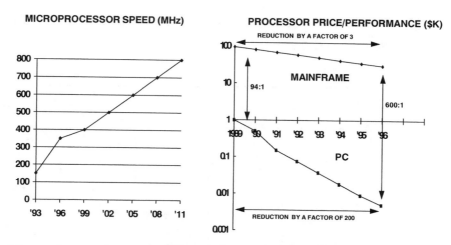

Figure 1.2   Microprocessor performance trends. Microprocessor price/performance trends favor client/server computing. (Source: *Practical Steps for Aligning Information Technology with Business Strategies,* Bernard H. Boar, John Wiley & Sons, Inc., 1994.)

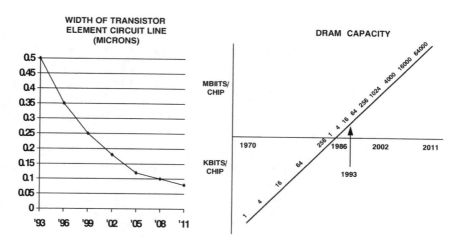

Figure 1.3   Memory performance trends. Memory price/performance trends favor client/server computing. (Source: *Practical Steps for Aligning Information Techology with Business Strategies,* Bernard H. Boar, John Wiley & Sons, Inc. 1994.)

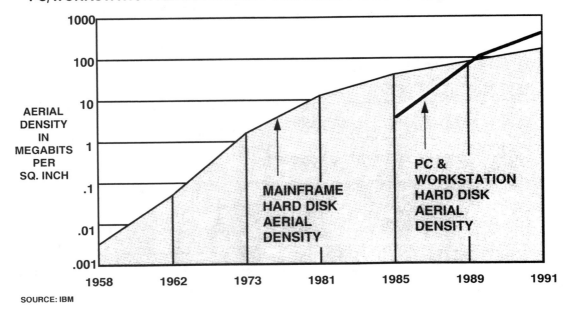

PC/WORKSTATION AERIAL DENSITY FOR HARD DISKS EXCEEDS MAINFRAMES

SOURCE: IBM

Figure 1.4   Storage performance trends. Storage price/performance trends favor client/server computing. (Source: IBM.)

- *Empowerment:* Client/server, with its ease of use, would permit end users to be much more self-sufficient.
- *Enterprise interoperability:* Client/server would permit the disparate corporate islands of I/T to be integrated.
- *Value chain interoperability:* Client/server would permit the business to interoperate with its trading partners.
- *Enterprise data access:* Client/server would permit the previously inaccessible stores of corporate data to be accessed by the people who needed the information when they needed it and how they needed it.
- *Vendor independence:* Built on standards, client/server would permit freedom from a single vendor.
- *Competitive advantage:* Client/server would permit novel applications to be built that would bring sustainable competitive advantage to the business.

It would be hard to imagine a more seductive scenario of motivations for adopting a new technology.

But just when you thought a client/server strategy was beyond question, safe, and even obvious, a minority but growing and eloquent cadre of consultants, gurus, market researchers, users, and vendors asserted that

- Client/server computing is significantly more expensive than mainframe computing and will continue to be so indefinitely.
- Client/server computing is not operationally manageable, for there are woefully inadequate tools to perform production quality operations, administration, and management (OA&M).
- Mainframe computing is the only architecture that provides adequate reliability, security, and integrity for production on-line transaction processing (OLTP) and operations support systems (OSS).
- Mainframe computing is neither dead nor a dinosaur but will experience not merely a revival but a renaissance.
- I/T and business executives have been oversold and fooled by the client/server hype of self-serving consultants and vendors.

Having been thought left for dead in the haste to client/server, Jason returned (Figure 1.5).

The group of sincere and concerned people who have taken these views are eclectic, and their individual positions vary widely. Some feel that client/server is good for nothing; others are surgically precise in their criticism. I refer to them, as a community, as the Mainframe Preservation Society (MPS). This reflects their shared core belief that the I/T community should indefinitely maintain (preserve) host-based computing as the predominant computing architecture (see Figure 1.6).

The following are unattributed quotations from the MPS. The selected extracts are from 17 different sources that are from the larger list in Appendix A. Though the material quoted is lengthy, it is necessary in order to fully appreciate the breadth of views of the MPS and their often irate attitude toward client/server computing.

IBM and all of you should be shot in the side of the head for allowing the mythology to be generated that mainframes are dead.... No one really understands the reasons for the move off the mainframe. Scores of companies continue to use mainframes to the fullest extent and accrue returns of hundreds of millions of dollars in technology investments.... In five years, these

Figure 1.5   **Jason returns. Just when we thought mainframe computing was dead and buried, like the movie character Jason
who won't die, it returns.**

client/server systems will be legacy systems themselves and I
wouldn't want to support them. . . . Client/server has staggering
support costs. C/S is twice as expensive to support as a comparative mainframe installation. The C/S promise of responsiveness
to corporate needs comes at too high a price. Mainframes offer
higher levels of reliability. . . .

Mainframe computing will grow 20% this year. Valuable applications are still clicking and whizzing away on mainframes. CSC
has difficulty meeting the functionality, data integrity or security
of a mainframe. The cost of a mainframe is not greater overall then
the cost of a CSC replacement once you add hidden costs. . . . C/S
will be more expensive than architectures are today. If customers
are anticipating saving money, they are nuts. . . . Vendors are
making transitions to alternative mainframes. Legacy applications

Figure 1.6 The Mainframe Preservation Society. As it has been it will be and as it will be it has been.

still have great value. Mainframes can run jobs that clog a PC for days. Mainframes can read and reuse the vast warehouse of old data that vast organizations have accumulated. I reject the notion that moving to distributed computing saves money. The traditional mainframe is dead, long live the mainframe. . . .

A widespread misconception is that CSC costs less than traditional host based computing. Distributed computing is four times more labor intensive. . . . For most large enterprises, adopting C/S will represent an increase in I/T spending. Client/sever computing is a labor intensive activity. Over time technology costs will continue to decline while labor costs will increase thereby exacerbating the problem. . . . Total costs/transaction is considerably lower for mainframe based applications than for PC-LAN based applications (14.3-1). Fewer than 1 in 10 US based companies are aware of PC-LAN costs or make a sincere effort to control them. Organizations are doing very little real downsizing from mainframes to PC-LANS. You cannot build large OLTP systems on PC-LANS. . . . The five year costs of applications deployed on LANS can be up to 300% greater than costs of mainframe centric applications. The bloated costs of client/server computing are becoming so obvious that they can no longer be ignored. C/S is an extravagant/expensive solution that offers nothing beyond some trendy intangibles and a negative return on investment. Mainframes not only refuse to die but seem in remarkably good health. Total installed mainframe MIPS grew 26.4%/annum from 1985–1993. What does the mainframe do better than LANs, almost everything. . . .

There are a lot of benefits to moving to client/server—but saving money is not one of them. Client/server will be 50% to 300% more expensive than mainframe systems. An average mainframe installation delivers 3 times faster response time. The average cost of a mainframe transaction was 3 cents/transaction while it was 43 cents/transaction for the PC/LAN. . . The 5 year costs of applications deployed on LANs are 1.5 to 2.8 higher than the costs of mainframe centric applications. . . . We are moving off mainframes but do not know why. We suspect it (moving to client/server computing) is a combination of "Airline Magazine Syndrome," guerrilla vendors (especially those with no mainframe expertise), PC magazines, and consultants in the seminar business. . . . Arguments for eliminating any future investment in mainframe technology are weak. LAN based C/S applications will cost at least 2 to 3 times what a mainframe costs. . . . The purported cost savings of mainframe alternatives evaporate when confronted with real world workloads and service requirements. Not only are PCs and LANs not a lower cost alternative to mainframe computing, in most cases, they are no alternative at all. It is increasingly difficult to ignore the savings that come from recentralization.

The MPS is certainly neither reserved nor shy in their critique of client/server computing.

Without question, the most well reasoned and best written defense of mainframe computing and criticism of client/server computing is *The Dinosaur Myth: Why the mainframe is the cheapest solution for most organizations.*[1] This 27-page white paper presents in seemingly impeccable logic the primary arguments of the MPS. Its essential points are as follows:

- The mainframe is the cheapest solution for most organizations.
- Far from being obsolete, mainframes currently offer the most cost-effective facilities for all but the smallest organizations and will continue to do so for the foreseeable future.

- Nonproductive activities with PCs cost 2% of the US GNP last year.
- Support for LANs costs 16 times more than their users suspect.
- Highly effective organizations have fewer PCs per worker than ineffective ones.
- Effective price/performance for LANs is actually static or declining.
- Downsizing has become a mindless fad.
- PC LANs are 67% more expensive than mainframes now and will be about the same in 1998.

This document is mandatory reading to fully appreciate the arguments of the MPS, and, as previously stated, it is the most concise and compelling statement of the MPS viewpoint that I have been able to find.

There is another eclectic group, The Proprietary System Conservation Society (PSCS), which, like its blood sibling, the MPS, is highly critical of client/server computing. However, its criticism is through indirection. The PSCS maintains the belief that standards based on open systems are a bad thing. The following are unattributed quotations from the PSCS that are extracted from the PSCS bibliography in Appendix B.

> It would be unwise to pay the cost penalty for open systems. It would be foolish in the extreme to commit to open systems. . . . Open standards are nothing more then attacking the market leader. . . . Over time, the facade of open systems will give way to account control and vendor lock-in. . . . Even if they were desirable, which I don't believe it is, [sic] I doubt open systems would be possible. . . The future will belong to proprietary systems created by entrepreneurs who refused to be bound. . . . Open systems are inferior to proprietary systems and always will be. . . . Open systems are a fantasy. . . . Open systems are a bureaucratic maze of acronyms and stop gap solutions.

Since the core of client/server benefits—interoperability, portability, scaleability, and reconfigurability—are standards based, the logic of the PSCS attack can be summarized in the following simple syllogism:

Client/server is dependent on open systems standards.
Open systems are neither possible nor desirable.

Client/server is neither possible nor desirable.

So what reminds those of us who were in the I/T industry during IBM's era of complete dominion, we have a grand return of FUD (fear, uncertainty, and doubt).

The chilling (to client/server advocates) united assertions of the MPS and the PSCS are then as follows:

- CSC is at best equal in cost to mainframe computing, may be as much as 14.3 times as expensive, and is most likely 3 or 4 times as expensive. This huge client/server cost penalty is due to "hidden costs" and huge labor costs. The situation will get markedly worse going forward.
- Open systems are at best bad and at worse undesirable. Since client/server is dependent on open systems, the interoperability and portability promised will never materialize.
- CSC is not production quality. It has a dearth of production quality OA&M tools and is therefore not suitable for "real" computing.
- Mainframe computing is alive and well. It stands poised on a new era of even greater accomplishment.
- The interest in client/server computing is entirely a function of the hollow hype and self-serving interests of client/server vendors, client/server consultants, and client/server media channels. No one really has a good reason for the move from mainframe computing to CSC.[2]

In *Wayne's World* language, the view of our MPS and PSCS colleagues is "Client/Server—NOT!"

Since billions of dollars for hardware, software, communications, training, facilities, and development are being diverted to client/server computing with elevated expectations, these assertions have very serious implications that should not be ignored. If you embrace these arguments, the following would seem adducible:

- Because I/T expenditures are from 1% to 4% (somewhat higher for I/T intensive industries) of revenue in a typical business, CSC at a cost of 3 to 14.3 times mainframe computing is clearly cost prohibitive. Client/server computing is not a strategy for the building of advantage but a strategy to drive your business bankrupt.
- Companies that are implementing CSC are taking extraordinary risks. How could you dare to implement a technology with so many OA&M shortcomings?

- Soon, IBM will again be $250/share and Microsoft, HP, Oracle, Compaq, Intel, AT&T, and so on will be in Chapter 11. The mainframe renaissance will result in a massive migration back to the data center, and the vendors of hollow client/server computing will get their just rewards in this world.
- I/T decision makers are mindless puppets who are easily manipulated by vendors and analysts. Since the average I/T decision maker has neither strategic acumen nor a deep understanding of information technology, vendors and analysts can pretty much say whatever they please and the foolish herd will follow these arrogant Pied Pipers anywhere.

We, therefore, are forced to confront the unbearable questions:

- Is CSC just another I/T fad that has peaked before it even happened?
- Have the billions of dollars spent by corporations throughout the world on migrating to CSC been an unpardonable waste?
- Is I/T management mindless, rash, and careless?
- Why are you moving to CSC?
- Is CSC not even good nonsense?

In other words, should your I/T strategy be to refocus your I/T investments on the mainframe and abandon, with all due haste, CSC?

The general response to the pincer attack of the MPS and the PSCS by the CSC community has been meek. They have ignored it, denied it, challenged it, and disparaged it, but the responses have been, on the whole, disappointingly shallow.[3] There has been an absence of a deep and far-reaching strategic refutation of these fallacious assertions.

Why the proponents and champions of CSC have been so reserved in their answer to the MPS is admittedly perplexing. The absence of a strong rebuttal indicates, at least to some, tacit agreement with the MPS assertions. I believe the problem is partly due to the complexity and size of a meaningful strategic refutation. While the MPS accusations are short, piercing, and pithy, and superficially appear eminently logical, a proper response requires the development of more sophisticated arguments. It is not only necessary to directly respond to each point, it is first necessary to preface the response with teaching/reviewing the logic of strategy. If the broad I/T community were already well versed in strategic thinking, the MPS assertions would long ago have been dismissed and discredited for the nonsense they are and a formal response would be superfluous.

Given an I/T media that prizes articles no longer than a single column and public seminar presentations of 60 minutes, formulating a mass market response is not easy. Consequently, you should be forewarned that the responses that are centered in Chapters 2 to 4 are thought-provoking and require reflection and study. If you are not prepared to first understand I/T and CSC strategically, you will not be able to evaluate and value the refutation.

My response to the MPS and the PSCS twins is that since the introduction of the IBM 360 architecture in 1964, there has not been an information technology as strategically important to the business as client/server computing. Those who understand client/server computing strategically will proceed with its implementation with complete confidence and ignore the rantings of the MPS and the PSCS. Those who implement client/server computing strategically will reap benefits far beyond any they could ever harvest with mainframe computing. The ideas of the MPS are "shallow and near-sighted" and will lead you to ruin.

The remaining essays in this book will serve as a strategic refutation to the MPS arguments and, in so doing, provide a path for an optimum implementation of CSC. Before doing that, however, it is necessary to clarify what is meant by host-based computing and client/server computing. Client/server computing is a processing model wherein a single application is partitioned among multiple processors (front-end and back-end) and the processors cooperate (transparent to the user) to complete the processing activity as a single unified task. A client/server bond product (middleware) glues the processors together to create a single system image (an illusion of one). Shareable resources are positioned as servers offering one or more services to needy clients. Applications are positioned as clients which access authorized servers and services. The entire architecture is endlessly recursive. In turn, servers can take the role of clients and request services from other servers on the network and so on and so on.

Figures 1.7 and 1.8 conceptually illustrate a client/server environment. The environment has the following attributes:

- It is multiprocessor oriented.
- Interoperability, portability, scaleability, and reconfigurability are primary features.

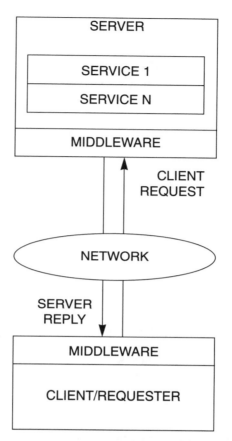

Figure 1.7   Client/server computing. The basic client/server architecture consist of a client processor and a server processor tied together transparently by middleware. (Source: *Implementing Client/Server Computing,* Bernard H. Boar, McGraw-Hill, 1993.)

- It is software centric. Software functionality is divided into three layers, presentation (PN), processing (PR—a.k.a. the function or logic layer), and data (DT), which are dispersed across the clients and servers in the most opportune fashion.
- It is open systems and standards oriented.
- The components are from heterogeneous vendors.
- Computing intelligence is dispersed to where it makes the most business sense.
- Configuration management is a horizontal problem.
- The I/T organization is in the systems integration business.

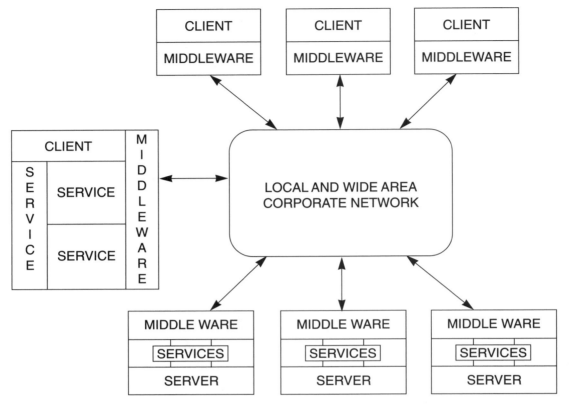

Figure 1.8   **Client and servers. A client/server environment would consist of clients, servers, clients and servers and an enterprise network. (Source: *Implementing Client/Server Computing*, Bernard H. Boar, McGraw-Hill, 1993.)**

Figure 1.9 illustrates the 32 basic client/server architectures that are derivable based on how you disperse PN, PR, and DT software layers. It is from this granular partitioning capability that the strategic business advantages of client/server emanate.

It is a little more difficult to define what exactly is meant by host-centered computing (a.k.a. mainframe computing or monolithic computing). The term is used very ambiguously by its advocates, but I believe it means a proprietary software and hardware architecture, provided primarily by a single vendor, wherein PN, PR, and DT software layers all run on the same processor (see Figure 1.10) and are often bundled. Some MPS enthusiasts

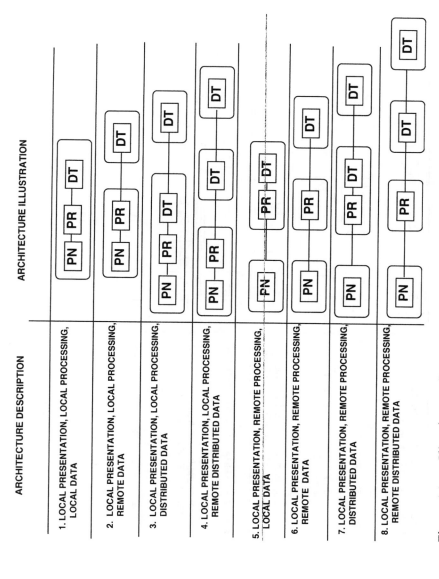

ARCHITECTURE DESCRIPTION

ARCHITECTURE ILLUSTRATION

1. LOCAL PRESENTATION, LOCAL PROCESSING, LOCAL DATA

2. LOCAL PRESENTATION, LOCAL PROCESSING, REMOTE DATA

3. LOCAL PRESENTATION, LOCAL PROCESSING, DISTRIBUTED DATA

4. LOCAL PRESENTATION, LOCAL PROCESSING, REMOTE DISTRIBUTED DATA

5. LOCAL PRESENTATION, REMOTE PROCESSING, LOCAL DATA

6. LOCAL PRESENTATION, REMOTE PROCESSING, REMOTE DATA

7. LOCAL PRESENTATION, REMOTE PROCESSING, DISTRIBUTED DATA

8. LOCAL PRESENTATION, REMOTE PROCESSING, REMOTE DISTRIBUTED DATA

Figure 1.9   Client/server flavors. Client/server computing comes in 32 basic architectures. (Source: *Practical Steps for Aligning Information Technology with Business Strategies,* Bernard H. Boar, John Wiley & Sons, Inc., 1994.)

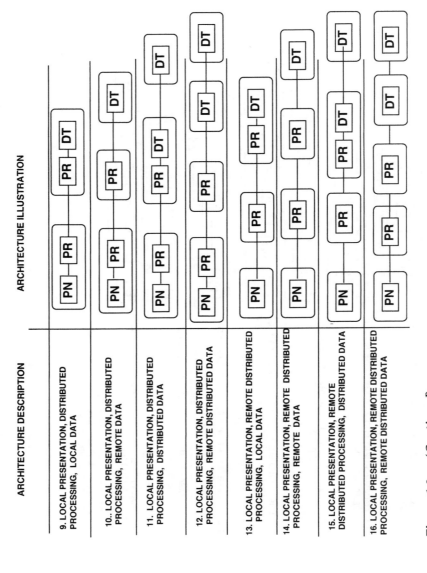

ARCHITECTURE DESCRIPTION

ARCHITECTURE ILLUSTRATION

9. LOCAL PRESENTATION, DISTRIBUTED PROCESSING, LOCAL DATA

10. LOCAL PRESENTATION, DISTRIBUTED PROCESSING, REMOTE DATA

11. LOCAL PRESENTATION, DISTRIBUTED PROCESSING, DISTRIBUTED DATA

12. LOCAL PRESENTATION, DISTRIBUTED PROCESSING, REMOTE DISTRIBUTED DATA

13. LOCAL PRESENTATION, REMOTE DISTRIBUTED PROCESSING, LOCAL DATA

14. LOCAL PRESENTATION, REMOTE DISTRIBUTED PROCESSING, REMOTE DATA

15. LOCAL PRESENTATION, REMOTE DISTRIBUTED PROCESSING, DISTRIBUTED DATA

16. LOCAL PRESENTATION, REMOTE DISTRIBUTED PROCESSING, REMOTE DISTRIBUTED DATA

Figure 1.9   (*Continued*)

16

ARCHITECTURE ILLUSTRATION

ARCHITECTURE DESCRIPTION

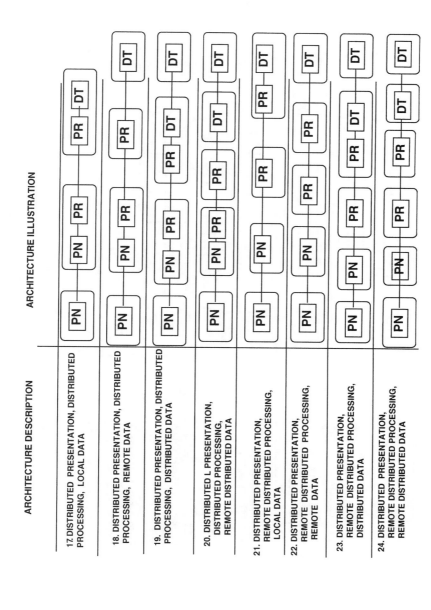

17. DISTRIBUTED PRESENTATION, DISTRIBUTED PROCESSING, LOCAL DATA

18. DISTRIBUTED PRESENTATION, DISTRIBUTED PROCESSING, REMOTE DATA

19. DISTRIBUTED PRESENTATION, DISTRIBUTED PROCESSING, DISTRIBUTED DATA

20. DISTRIBUTED L PRESENTATION, DISTRIBUTED PROCESSING, REMOTE DISTRIBUTED DATA

21. DISTRIBUTED PRESENTATION, REMOTE DISTRIBUTED PROCESSING, LOCAL DATA

22. DISTRIBUTED PRESENTATION, REMOTE DISTRIBUTED PROCESSING, REMOTE DATA

23. DISTRIBUTED PRESENTATION, REMOTE DISTRIBUTED PROCESSING, DISTRIBUTED DATA

24. DISTRIBUTED PRESENTATION, REMOTE DISTRIBUTED PROCESSING, REMOTE DISTRIBUTED DATA

Figure 1.9 (*Continued*)

17

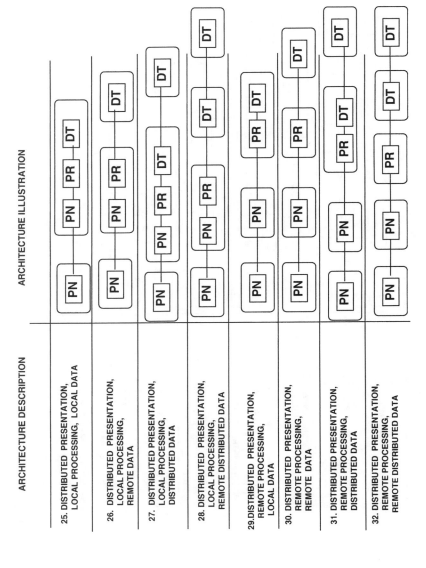

ARCHITECTURE DESCRIPTION

ARCHITECTURE ILLUSTRATION

25. DISTRIBUTED PRESENTATION, LOCAL PROCESSING, LOCAL DATA

26. DISTRIBUTED PRESENTATION, LOCAL PROCESSING, REMOTE DATA

27. DISTRIBUTED PRESENTATION, LOCAL PROCESSING, DISTRIBUTED DATA

28. DISTRIBUTED PRESENTATION, LOCAL PROCESSING, REMOTE DISTRIBUTED DATA

29. DISTRIBUTED PRESENTATION, REMOTE PROCESSING, LOCAL DATA

30. DISTRIBUTED PRESENTATION, REMOTE PROCESSING, REMOTE DATA

31. DISTRIBUTED PRESENTATION, REMOTE PROCESSING, DISTRIBUTED DATA

32. DISTRIBUTED PRESENTATION, REMOTE PROCESSING, REMOTE DISTRIBUTED DATA

Figure 1.9   (*Continued*)

18

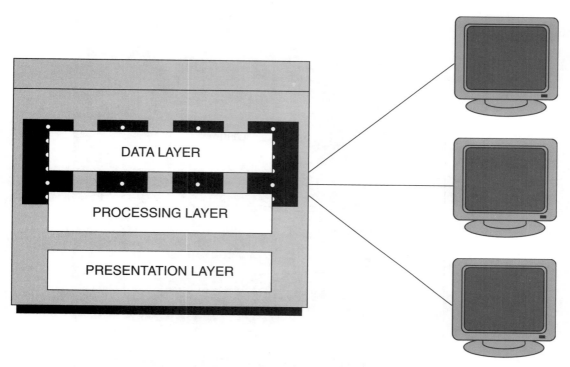

Figure 1.10   Host-centered computing. Mainframe computing is characterized by the PN, PR, and DT layers all coexisting on the same processor.

would permit the presentation layer to be distributed while others would argue that mainframes can and do function perfectly well as PR or DT "servers." The environment has the following attributes:

- It is hardware centric (i.e., "Big Iron").
- Computing is data-center centered.
- It is proprietary.
- It is homogeneous, dominated by a primary hardware vendor (see Figure 1.11).
- There is little portability, scaleability, interoperability, or reconfigurability.
- Clients are dumb.

Traditional mainframes are evolving into network servers with client/server feature/functionality (i.e., openness, portability,

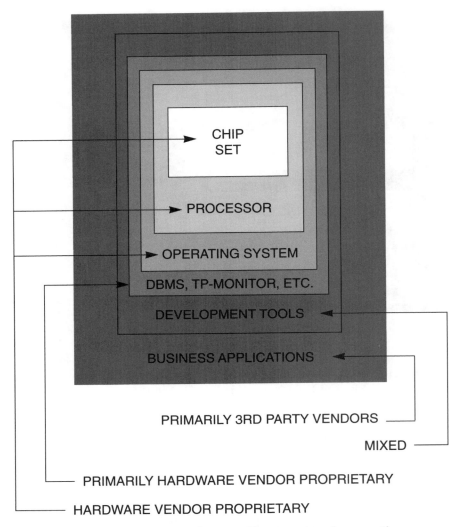

Figure 1.11   **Proprietary architecture. The inner layers of host-centered computing were provided primarily by the hardware vendor. (Source:** *Practical Steps for Aligning Information Technology with Business Strategies,* **Bernard H. Boar, John Wiley & Sons, Inc., 1994.)**

scaleability, etc.). However, when a mainframe transforms itself into an open server, it is no longer participating in a mainframe architecture but has switched sides and joined the client/server architecture community. I will therefore stick with the view that what the MPS means is a proprietary software and hardware architecture provided primarily by a single vendor wherein PN, PR, and DT software layers (except perhaps presentation) all run on the same processor.[4]

I would like to end this essay by clarifying my use of the Mainframe Preservation Society and Proprietary Systems Conservation Society appellations. Some people have interpreted them as being disparaging and derisive. That certainly was not my intent. My intent was to assign a name that was factually accurate and, perhaps, even a little humorous. Nevertheless, to show my egalitarian spirit, I will assign a label to the proponents of client/server computing. I will call them the Client/Server Peoples Liberation Army (CSPLA). Now, onto the rebuttal!

NOTES

1. *The Dinosaur Myth*, Second Edition, Xephon PLC.
2. I suspect that if the MPS prevails, I and other client/server consultant advocates, like the shamed heroine Hester Prynne of Hawthorne's most famous novel, *The Scarlet Letter*, will be condemned to wear the scarlet letters "C/S" on our lapels as contrition for our unpardonable sins against host-centered computing.
3. For an example of a response to the MPS, see "System Cost Analysis Might Be Start of Client/Server Backlash," *Infoworld*, 5/10/93.
4. We need to make a subtle distinction. There is a difference between a mainframe computer and mainframe computing architecture. A mainframe computer, like any computer, depending on what hardware, software, and communications capabilities are provided, could participate as a client or server in a client/server environment. A mainframe computing architecture or monolithic host-centered computing architecture, as we have described it, refers to the partitioning of software function across computers and the cooperative delivery of services across those computers. Our argument with the MPS is an architecture argument, not a computer argument. The benefits they cite for mainframe computing are benefits rooted in architecture. Who will be the clients and who will be the servers is a question of cost and value. My interpretation of the MPS literature is that they are opposed to a client/server architecture regardless of who is the client and who is the server.

2

Corporate Strategy, Information Technology, and Client/Server Computing

For at least the last 15 years, one of the most persistent and stubborn problems that has confronted the I/T community has been the problem of strategically aligning information technology investments and initiatives with business strategy. Numerous studies throughout the world have repeatedly identified the absence of I/T–business alignment as one of the primary causes of dissatisfaction by the business leadership with their I/T assets. This dissatisfaction is not surprising: If you are misaligned your energies are depleted wastefully struggling among yourselves rather then serving the customer or defeating the competition. Coordination, tenacity, and concentration of effort toward a shared set of objectives, alignment, is the most fundamental strategic necessity for any business.[1]

The problem is not intractable, and we would like to address the problem of how to align I/T with business strategy by speaking to two questions sequentially:

1. How should the I/T organization be structured to perfectly align with the corporate structure and strategy of a global multi-business (i.e., multiple strategic business unit) corporation?
2. How, if at all, does client/server computing contribute to I/T–business alignment?

By a strategic business unit (SBU), we mean a self-contained and partitioned business within a corporation that

- Is a collection of related businesses.
- Has a distinct mission.

23

- Serves a clear set of markets.
- Has a clear set of competitors.
- Has the resources, products, and value chain constructs to deliver competitive products and services to the customer.
- Has a distinct management team.
- Has profitability responsibility.

In a large corporation there will be a corporate office and from 2 to n strategic business units. For I/T to be aligned, it must be aligned with both the corporate strategy and the strategies of the multiple SBUs.

CORPORATE STRATEGY

The highest-level strategy of a business is its corporate business strategy. At the corporate level, the senior leadership must develop strategy by addressing the following business character defining questions:

1. What industries (products, customers, and geographical markets) will the company compete in?
2. What are the performance objectives for the enterprise? What is winning?
3. How will the SBUs be partitioned and what will be the degree of independence and collaboration among them?
4. How will finite resources be divided across the SBUs?
5. How will we attract and retain the best possible staff?
6. What will be the basis for competing and competitive advantage? How will we win?

In this way, the corporate leadership addresses at the macro level the key stakeholder issues of customers, owners, and employees and the problem of competition.

The collective answers to those six questions define a strategic position for the corporation along a continuum between a "union" strategy and a "multistate" strategy (see Figure 2.1). A union strategy means that the enterprise, as a whole, will maximize performance and growth through extensive sharing, collaboration, and leverage across SBUs. A multistate strategy means that the enter-

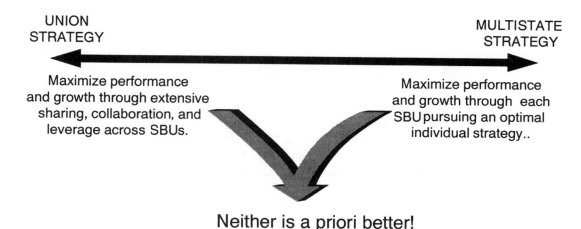

UNION
STRATEGY

MULTISTATE
STRATEGY

Maximize performance
and growth through extensive
sharing, collaboration, and
leverage across SBUs.

Maximize performance
and growth through each
SBU pursuing an optimal
individual strategy..

Neither is a priori better!

Figure 2.1   Union strategy and multistate strategy. A corporate strategy is chosen somewhere along this continuum.

prise, as a whole, will maximize performance and growth by each SBU pursuing an optimal individual SBU centric strategy. Neither strategy, union or multistate, is a priori superior; what should be chosen is a function of the specific facts of each situation.

The answer to corporate strategy question 6, "What will be the basis for competing and competitive advantage? How will we win?" has a disproportionate strong influence on the union or multistate decision. To answer this question, the following four issues must be analyzed:

1. *Market Position:* To what extent do market segments across SBUs and product lines overlap? To what extent will the businesses share brand names, advertising, customer image, and other marketing elements across product and market?
2. *Products/Services Position:* To what extent is there synergy across SBU product lines?
3. *Competitive Moves:* To what extent is advantage accrued by linking and coordinating competitive aggressive and defensive moves across SBUs?
4. *Cost Position:* To what extent does cross-SBU collaboration lead to cost advantage (i.e., reuse, leverage, economies of scale, economies of scope, economies of sharing, and economies of learning)?

The answers to these questions are not easily derived, but these answers drive the union-multistate decision.

There are many analytical frameworks that can be used to assist in answering these questions. Four frameworks are as follows:

1. *Cost, Differentiation, and Market Focus* (Figure 2.2): Competitive theory indicates that there are four basic ways to compete: low-cost leader, value added/differentiation, low cost and narrow market focus, and value added/differentiation and narrow market focus. As shown in Figure 2.2, a cost strategy tends to push one to a union strategy, while a differentiation strategy tends to push one to a multistate strategy. This would logically make

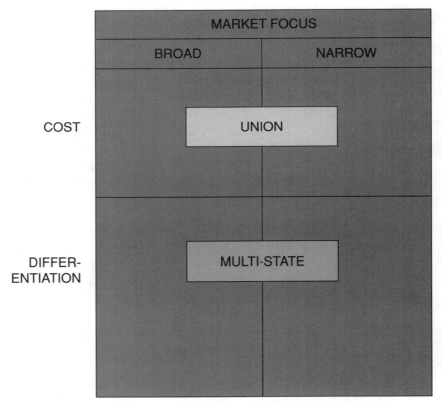

Figure 2.2   **Cost, differentiation, and focus. A cost strategy is most sympathetic to a union strategy, whereas a differentiation strategy is most sympathetic to a multistate strategy.**

sense because the more you compete on differentiation, the more important it is for each SBU to be free to quickly meet the specific needs of its customers without the consensus of others.

2. *Products and Processes* (Figure 2.3): Products and processes may be viewed as stable or dynamic. As shown in Figure 2.3, stability promotes a union strategy, while dynamics promotes a multistate strategy. This would logically make sense because the more dynamic the situation, the freer each business unit must be to rapidly respond to its specific dynamics without requiring agreement from nonimpacted SBUs.

3. *Measures of SBU Performance* (Figure 2.4): Common measurements that are used to measure SBU leadership are market performance (change in market share and absolute market share),

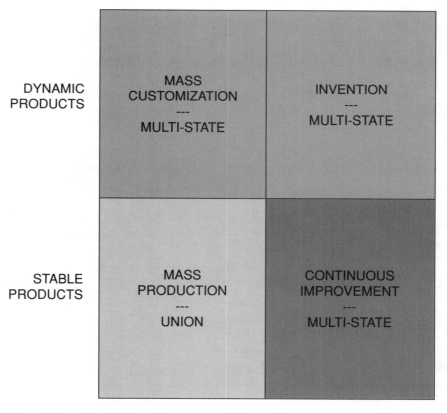

Figure 2.3   **Products and processes. Dynamics support a multistate strategy, whereas stability supports a union strategy.**

SBU	EFFECTIVENESS	EFFICIENCY	ADAPTABILITY
	MARKET SHARE	ROI/EVA	% REVENUE NEW PRODUCTS
SBU1			
SBU2			
SBU3			
SBUn			

Figure 2.4   Measures of SBU performance. Common measures of performance support a union strategy, whereas different ordered measures of performance support a multistate strategy.

efficiency (return on investment, economic value added, etc.) and adaptability (percentage of revenue from new products/services [less than 3 years old]). As shown in Figure 2.4, to each SBU an order of measurement may be assigned. The priority order of the measurements will strongly influence SBU leadership behavior. If the orders of measurement are similar across SBUs, than a union strategy would be indicated. Conversely, if the orders of measurement are different across SBUs, a multistate strategy is indicated. This makes logical sense because if you attempt a union strategy with SBUs that are being driven by different priorities of measures, their behaviors will obviously be quite different and will conflict.

4. *SBU Market Mix Compatibility* (Figure 2.5): Each SBU has a market ambition (dominate, attack, hold, defend, retreat, harvest, abandon) and a corresponding set of marketing elements to achieve that ambition. If one defines the elements for each SBU and they are similar, a union strategy would be indicated. The more they diverge, the more a multistate strategy is indicated.

SBU	MARKET AMBITION	PRODUCT	PROMOTION	PRICE	PROCESS	PEOPLE
SBU1						
SBU2						
SBU3						
SBUn						

Figure 2.5 SBU market mix. Similar market mixes support a union strategy, whereas different market mixes support a multistate strategy.

The logic of this is that if the marketing ambitions and elements are in conflict, there is no basis for a union. How can you engage in a union if the market styles are incompatible?

There are of course numerous other analytical and synthesis frameworks that can be used to support the decision-making process. They all reduce to trying to understand commonalities and dissimilarities in terms of customers, products, rewards, and actions.

In practice, corporate strategy definition is very complex. A pure union or pure multistate strategy is neat, clean, and easy to understand but is atypical. Corporate strategy is often a moving point along the continuum (Figure 2.1). There may be multiple clusters of "union" SBUs, and independent SBUs may selectively cooperate. For explanatory purposes, we will assume a pure union or multistate strategy.

Figure 2.6 summarizes the logic of developing a corporate strategy. While most people would intuitively vote for a union strategy, in reality, a union strategy is a very difficult decision. The fundamental concept in the identification of strategic business units is to identify the discrete independent product/market segments served by the firm. The idea is to partition based on discrete strategic market elements. A corporate union strategy may inherently

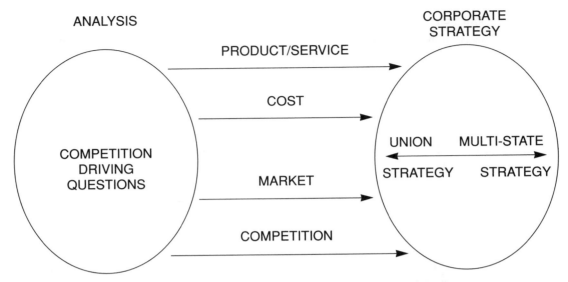

Figure 2.6 **Corporate strategy logic. Corporate strategy is driven by the answers to six question but in particular the issue of how the business will compete.**

contradict the fundamental logic of strategic business units. If we are to be a strong union, why are we separate business units in the first place? Since a union strategy is intrinsically more complicated (it requires additional coordination and collaboration), the onus should be to prove why a multistate strategy is not correct. Why overlay additional complexity, effort, and cost unless there are demonstrated countervailing benefits?

STRATEGIC BUSINESS UNIT STRATEGY

With the corporate strategy defined, each resultant SBU is itself confronted with the same questions of market position, product/service position, competitive moves, and cost position that had to be addressed at the macro corporate level but now must be addressed at the intra-SBU product line level (see Figure 2.7). Will the product lines within an SBU confront the marketplace with a union or a multistate strategy? Again, numerous methods of analysis and synthesis are available to help answer this question. One would expect a SBU to normally choose a union strategy across product lines. Since SBUs are defined by common strategic market elements, we should

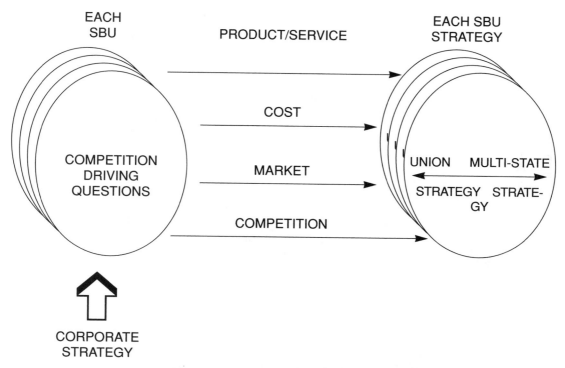

Figure 2.7   SBU strategy logic. Each SBU has to also decide how it will compete.

anticipate that an SBU would fight as an entity; if not, why did we make it an SBU?

We can now see how corporate strategy and SBU strategy may align. As shown in Figure 2.8, there are four choices:

1. *A Union/Union Strategy* (Figure 2.8: Cell 1): SBUs will extensively collaborate with each other in terms of products, markets, costs, competencies, processes, and so on.
2. *Union/Multistate Strategy* (Figure 2.8: Cell 2): This combination represents misalignment. If we are to compete at a corporate strategic level as a union, it is contradictory to compete at the SBU product line levels as independent states.
3. *Multistate/Union Strategy* (Figure 2.8: Cell 3): SBUs will optimize their own market success by extensive collaboration across each SBU's product lines.

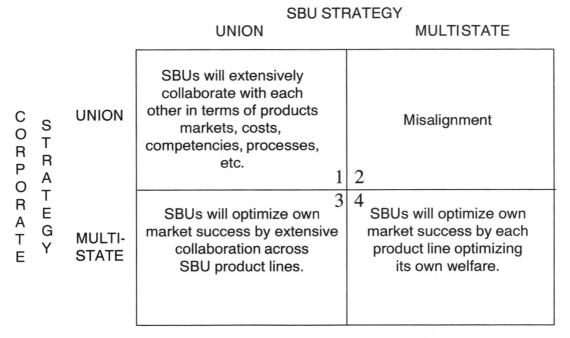

Figure 2.8   Cooperate/SBU Alignment. Of the four possible ways of alignment, one is fundamentally a misaligned condition and must be avoided.

4. *Multistate/Multistate Strategy* (Figure 2.8: Cell 4): SBUs will optimize own market success by each product line optimizing its own welfare.

In this way, there is harmony between corporate and SBU strategy. Now that we understand how corporate strategy and SBU strategy can be aligned, we can turn our attention to the first question we originally asked, "How should the I/T organization be structured to perfectly align with the corporate structure and strategy of a global multibusiness (i.e., multiple strategic business unit) corporation?"

I/T ORGANIZATION STRUCTURE

Sun Tzu said, "Structure depends on strategy. Forces are to be structured strategically based on what is advantageous." The I/T structure problem is summarized in Figure 2.9. Given a corpo-

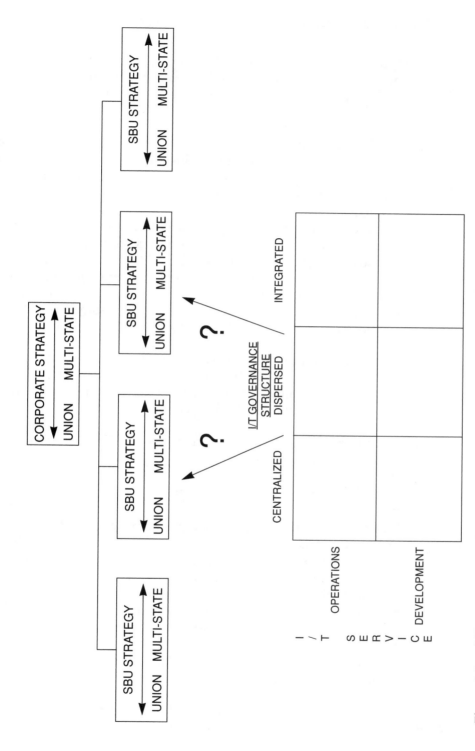

Figure 2.9   I/T structure. The problem of I/T structure is that of aligning an I/T governance mechanism for development and operations with the corporate/SBU strategy.

rate/SBU strategy combination, how should I/T services and governance structure be overlaid on the union/multistate decision?

There are two basic services that the I/T community provides to its clients:

1. *Application Development:* This embraces life-cycle application development and maintenance. This includes but is not limited to analysis, design, development, maintenance, systems integration, architecture, and solutions consulting.
2. *Production Operations:* This embraces the operations, administration, and maintenance (OA&M) of both the I/T infrastructure (platform) and the business applications that execute on that infrastructure. Functions included in OA&M are service management, configuration management, job management, fault management, security administration, backup and recovery, and disaster recovery. Table 2.1 summarizes standard OA&M functions at both the infrastructure and application levels.

The two, development and operations, are independent though related services, and should be allocated separately.[2]

Figure 2.10 illustrates the three basic governance structures that may be chosen for both development and operations:

1. *Centralized:* One global group manages I/T. The corporate I/T organization is very strong. The strong positive of this choice is economies of scale. The strongest negative is bureaucracy and lack of responsiveness. I/T architecture in this structure is centralized.
2. *Dispersed:* Multiple independent groups provide I/T services to distinct customers. Corporate I/T is weak. The strong positive of this choice is focus and effectiveness. The strongest negative is cost economies. I/T architecture in this structure is dispersed.
3. *Integrated:* Services are provided by separate but coordinated groups. Corporate I/T in this alternative is a partner. The strongest positive of this solution is collaboration; the strongest negative is politics. I/T architecture is a governance mechanism, as it provides the rules of exchange of information across the independent but coordinated entities.

Again, as illustrated in Figure 2.9, the I/T structure problem is deciding, for both development and operations, what governance

Table 2.1
OA&M Functions.

OA&M Level	Function	Examples
Application	Software Release Management	Distribution, installation, testing, change control, backout, intersite coordination
	Monitoring	Component connectivity, message movement, file transfer completion
	Performance Management	Proactive prevention, trend analysis, tuning, bottleneck resolution, trending
	Change Management	Application movement, topology management, directory maintenance
	Backup/Restore	Full/incremental backup/restore, media management, off-site archival storage
	Database Administration	Space management, permissions, restart, sizing
	Security Administration	User Id and password administration, incident tracking
	Help Desk	User query resolution
	Job Management	Batch job setup, scheduling, monitoring, output distribution
Infrastructure (Platform)	Configuration Management	Provisioning, system software distribution, installation, directory management, name management, change management
	Fault Management	help desk, trouble identification and tracking, tired support, problem isolation and resolution
	Performance Management	Measurement, tracking, tuning
	Security Management	Access permissions, violation monitoring, permission levels
	Accounting utilization	Billing Ids, billing, asset

Operations must provide all of these functions to the application users. (Source: *The Art of Strategic Planning for Information Technology*, Bernard H. Boar, John Wiley & Sons, 1993)

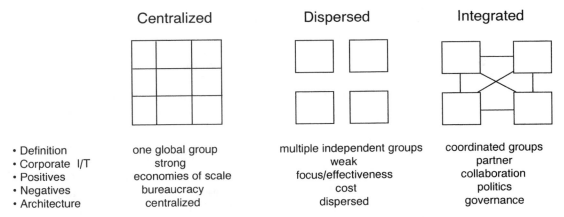

	Centralized	Dispersed	Integrated
• Definition	one global group	multiple independent groups	coordinated groups
• Corporate I/T	strong	weak	partner
• Positives	economies of scale	focus/effectiveness	collaboration
• Negatives	bureaucracy	cost	politics
• Architecture	centralized	dispersed	governance

Figure 2.10   I/T governance structures. There are three basic governance structures for the I/T organization.

mechanism should be allocated for each to best promote alignment of the I/T assets with the corporate/SBU strategy.

What should be done can be derived by analyzing the information flow implications of the chosen corporate/SBU strategy (Figure 2.8):

1. *Union/Union Strategy* (Figure 2.8: Cell 1): SBUs will extensively collaborate with each other in terms of products markets, costs, competencies, processes, and so on. There will therefore be extensive collaboration, sharing, and cooperation between SBUs, which will demand extensive horizontal information flows across SBUs and to corporate staff.
2. *Union/Multistate Strategy* (Figure 2.8: Cell 2): This combination represents misalignment. If we are to compete at a corporate strategic level as a union, it is contradictory to compete at the SBU product line levels as independent states.
3. *Multistate/Union Strategy* (Figure 2.8: Cell 3): SBUs will optimize their own market success by extensive collaboration across each SBU's product lines. There will therefore be extensive collaboration, sharing, and cooperation within SBUs, which will demand extensive horizontal information flows within each SBU but limited information flows between SBUs and to corporate staff.
4. *Multistate/Multistate Strategy* (Figure 2.8: Cell 4): SBUs will optimize own market success by each product line optimizing its

own welfare. There will therefore be extensive collaboration, sharing, and cooperation within SBU product lines, which would indicate limited horizontal information flows within each SBU, between SBUs, and to corporate staff.

Using these implications, Figures 2.11 and 2.12 show possible aligned and misaligned solutions for structuring the I/T organizations. The trick is to choose a governance structure that is in harmony with the information flows of the corporate/SBU strategy combination and enhances the strategy.

In practice, the I/T assets are often misaligned. The reasons for this are as follows:

- Complexities of corporate/SBU strategy.
- The business changes faster then the I/T structure.
- A misunderstanding of the corporate/SBU strategy.

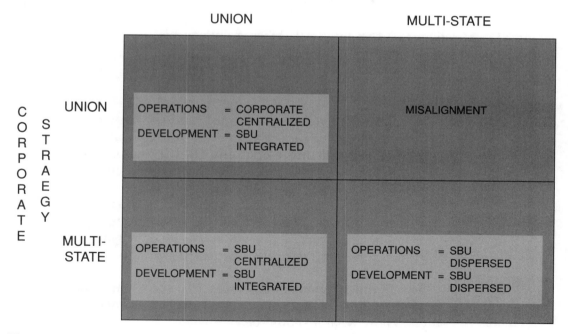

Figure 2.11   Aligned I/T structures. All of these solutions align I/T with the corporate/SBU strategy.

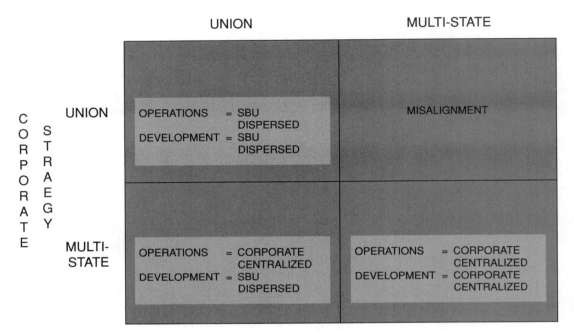

Figure 2.12   **Misaligned I/T structures. All of these solutions misalign I/T with the corporate/SBU strategy.**

- Contradictory strategy. A multistate/union strategy is promoted for the enterprise, but the I/T organization is given the mission to maximize economies of scale across the enterprise as its primary objective rather than to meet the distinct competitive needs of each SBU state.
- I/T is not considered a major corporate player and is ignored.
- Inertia of the existing structure resists alignment efforts.
- Politics. The current game players like things the way they are and don't wish to risk a restructuring.

Misalignment need not be the case. The problem is solvable, but, as we have just listed, there are many obstacles to achieving it even if you know what it should be.

We can summarize what we have learned to this point as follows:

- Corporate strategy can be modeled as a data point between a union and a multistate strategy.
- SBU strategy, with the corporate strategy given, can be modeled as a data point between a union and multistate strategy.
- An I/T governance structure of centralized, dispersed, or integrated strategies for both development and operations may be developed against the modeled (corporate strategy, SBU Strategy) pair.

In this way, we impose by design alignment between corporate strategy, SBU strategy, and I/T governance structure.

We can now turn our attention to the second question we asked originally, "How, if at all, does client/server computing contribute to I/T–business alignment?"

CLIENT/SERVER COMPUTING AND I/T–BUSINESS ALIGNMENT

The puzzle is as follows: Given a set of feasible strategies of the form (corporate strategy, SBU strategy, I/T governance structure),[3] is client/server always, sometimes, or never the preferred I/T architecture to maximize alignment? Given the choices shown in Figure 2.13, when would we choose one or the other? The answers to these questions strike at the heart of the debate with the MPS. The answer to the question of which architecture best promotes alignment is the strategic architecture decision driver.

For most organizations, especially now as we move into the information age, where knowledge becomes the basis of advantage in lieu of the traditional value holders of land, capital, and labor, the primary or first adjunct business process is the creation, processing, interpretation, and dissemination of information in all its forms. Organizations may therefore be interpreted as massively parallel human and automated information processing entities (Figure 2.14). The information assets are the underlying linchpins to both the short-term performance and the long-term growth of the business.

The core problem of information technology (I/T)–business alignment may therefore be understood as the problem of overlaying I/T flexibility on business environmental diversity (Figure 2.15). Flexibility is the ability of the I/T assets to maneuver (adapt, reconfigure, scale, restructure, be agile, etc.) to respond to business changes in a cost-efficient manner. Business environmental diversi-

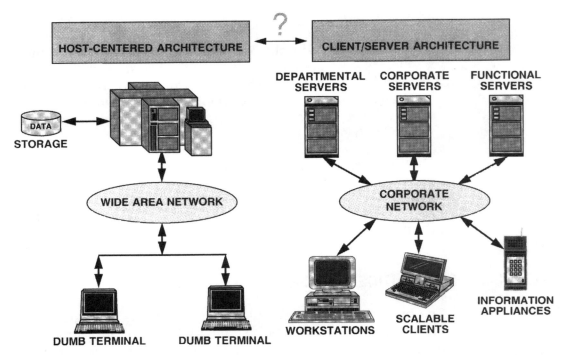

Figure 2.13   **CSC or monolithic host-based computing. Which architecture best supports I/T–business alignment? (Source:** *Implementing Client/Server Computing,* **Bernard H. Boar, McGraw-Hill, 1993.)**

ty is the complexity of the information exchange relationships within the business and between the business and its value chain partners. The strategic challenge of business I/T alignment, then, is to implement an I/T architecture that maximizes flexibility at the absolute minimum cost. This challenge is the same regardless of the triplet (corporate strategy, SBU strategy, I/T governance structure) selected. In addition, since the strategy triplet is subject to constant revision, flexibility of the I/T assets are necessary beyond the immediate and temporary triplet strategy so that a new strategy can be shifted to when and if required.

Figure 2.16 provides a view of the drivers of internal business environmental diversity. We refer to Figure 2.16 as a "business diversity box." Diversity is defined by four dimensions:

1. *Work Site Diversity:* What are the types of work site arrangements and the diverseness of their geography?

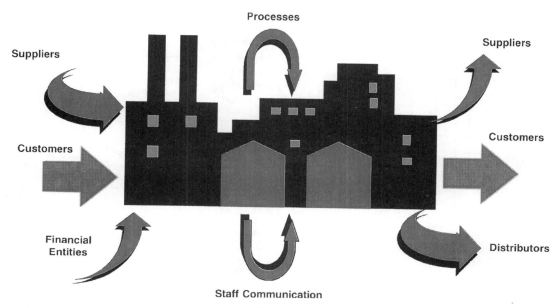

Figure 2.14   Organizations are massively parallel information-processing entities. A business can be viewed as an information factory.

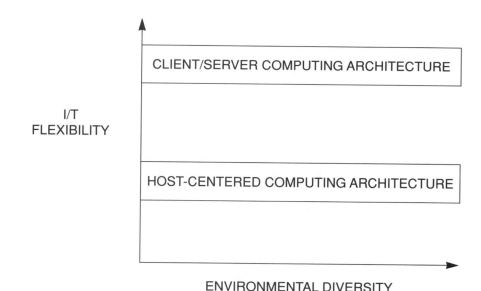

Figure 2.15   Overlaying information flexibility on business environmental diversity. The fundamental problem is to overlay a malleable I/T architecture on business information diversity.

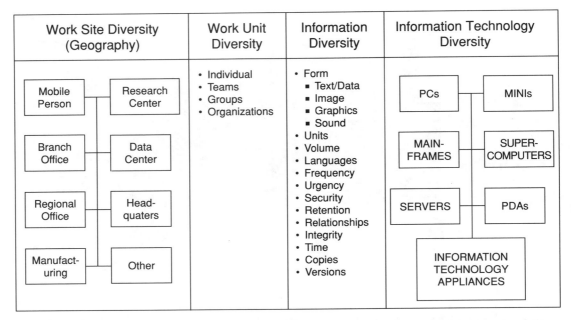

Figure 2.16   Business diversity box. The business diversity box highlights the elements that drive information flow diversity within a business.

2. *Work Unit Diversity:* What are the different types of collaborative work units?
3. *Information Diversity:* What are the different forms of information exchanged (sound, text, image/animation/video, graphics)? In what differing languages and units of expression (dollars vs. francs)? What is the variety of frequency and volume of exchange? How urgent is the need for the information to be received? How restricted must the dissemination of the information be? What are the retention requirements for the information? What other information does this information relate to? Must we be sure that the information is received? How many copies of the information exist? How many versions of the information exist? The challenge of managing information diversity is becoming even more exaggerated due to the *convergence* of all information forms into digitized format and the resulting ability to move and manage those information forms (text, audio, video, graphics) interactively on a set of interoperable computing platforms.

4. *Information Technology Diversity:* What are the different types of information technology devices that collect, present, store, move, exchange, and access information?

It should be obvious that within a business of any size there is an astronomical number of combinations and permutations of information flows resulting from these diversity drivers. Of more concern, the situation is dynamic and the diversity combinations and permutations are continually mutating in response to business turbulence. Competing globally has exacerbated this problem.

As illustrated in Figure 2.17, when one collocates the business diversity box into the value chain context with the business diversity boxes of its value chain trading partners (i.e., customers, suppliers, distributors, regulators, financiers, etc.), the complexity of information exchange due to environmental diversity becomes strikingly obvious. Numerous combinations of information flows must coexist. These flows are dynamic, distinct, and constantly in a state of flux, and there is always high uncertainty as to what new combinations of information flows will be needed, when they will be needed, and which existing flows will become vestigial.

These information flows encompass three generic types of business systems (transactions systems, decision support systems, and information exchange/collaboration systems). Information flows across the value chain undergo continuous and unpredictable reconfiguration with shifting combinations and permutations of diversity box participants both within the business and with value chain partners. Since the business is both internally and externally process and relationship driven, advantage accrues to those business that can more rapidly and creatively make and break information flow relationships. The dynamics of these information flows have become even more unpredictable and exaggerated because of the business turbulence that characterizes our era (i.e., global competition, mass customization, shortened product life cycles, environmentalism, diversity, the health insurance cost crisis, changing demographics, mergers and acquisitions, downsizings, and the extraordinary quest for continuing cost savings and productivity improvements).

As we have seen, the choice of strategy also can drastically impact information flows. A union/union strategy will accelerate the demands for information flows across the corporation. A multistate/union strategy will reduce the demands for inter-SBU infor-

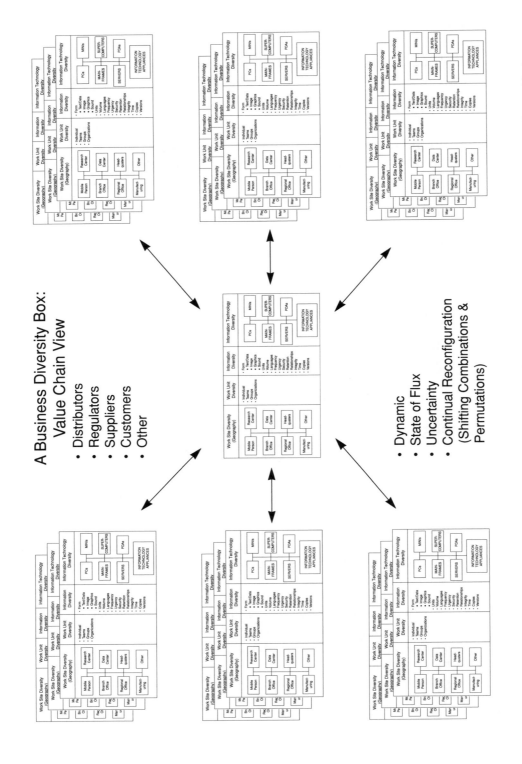

Figure 2.17 Business diversity box and the value chain. The problem of information exchange between business diversity boxes across the value chain.

mation flow but, if the SBU is competing based on differentiation, a great deal of information will need to be collected and shared to maintain foresighted sensitivity to evolving customer needs. In all cases, information flows with the external trading partners will grow as businesses move toward ever-increased electronic commerce as the primary means of economic and information exchange.

The way to respond and cope with "diversity in constant motion" is with flexibility. Flexibility is a rich concept and should be apprehended as follows:

- It is the qualities of a system that permit it to respond easily to change and variety.
- It is the robust ability to deal with variance.
- It is the capacity to take new and novel actions in response to new and novel circumstances.
- It is the ability to respond to environmental disruption without collapse or disorganization.
- It is the ability to add, modify, or delete without causing disruption.
- It is the ability to be agile and nimble in response to fluctuations.

An I/T architecture, A_1, is more flexible then another architecture, B_1, if the set of possible architectural choices available following architecture A_1 includes the set of possible architectural choices following architecture B_1.

Client/server computing is strategically important because it provides a high maneuverability architecture at a low cost[4] (Figure 2.18) that is able to respond to the dynamics, turbulence, and unpredictability of the value chain (Figure 2.17). Mainframe computing is expensive and offers absolute minimal flexibility to deal with the shifting information relationships of the value chain. The nature of mainframe computing is best captured in the phrase "one size fits all." With CSC, architecture takes on the quality of being "temporary" by design as opposed to being "fixed." It takes on the quality of being fluid instead of being solid.[5]

The strategic issue of I/T architecture as a means to I/T–business alignment, then, is as follows:

- The problem of aligning information technology should be understood as the challenge of the economical overlaying of

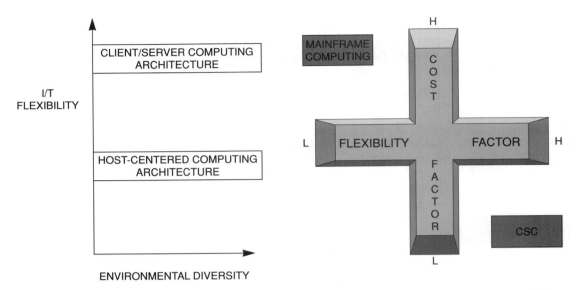

Figure 2.18 High flexibility and low cost. Client/server computing is a preferred architecture because it offers high flexibility at a low cost.

I/T flexibility upon a constantly shifting value chain with enormous diversity and unpredictability of information flows. We must blanket the environmental diversity with ever-greater I/T flexibility.

- The mainframe computing architecture is expensive, and, even more important, it is inflexible.
- Client/server computing offers extraordinary adaptability to the management and deployment of I/T assets. The I/T assets become formless, like water; they can be moved, added, or changed to quickly cope with the shifting diversity but maintain a constant transparent interface to the nonimpacted user community. Nondisruptive change can take place with alacrity. CSC is preferable because it will permit the business in a world of increasing torrid global competition to maneuver with unparalleled swiftness.

As a consequence of this, there are significant strategic implications from the decision to migrate to a client/server architecture from a monolithic host-centered computing architecture:

- The business management has more choices of strategic actions. The degrees of strategic freedom have been markedly increased.

- You are free to experiment. Since you are fast and agile, prototyping and pathfinder projects become the normal means for testing and validating ideas. You truly can become a learning organization.
- The complexity of value chain relationships can be altered and, therefore, can become the basis for new advantages. You can design sophisticated acts of collaboration that your competitors cannot duplicate that result in delighting customers. You can further prevent your competitors from copying you and obtaining competitive parity by using the I/T flexibility to periodically improve and reshape the value chain. The ability to increase the tempo of value chain arrangements will further unsettle your competitors' response abilities.
- Your startup times shrink. You therefore have reduced time to action.
- Your reaction times decrease. You therefore can quickly parry the actions of your competitors
- Because of these three items, you become a more attractive value chain partner for future trading partners at all ends of the chain. You can build relationship-based advantages.
- Information has increased value. It has increased value because it can be accessed, because it can shared, and, most important, because it can be acted upon in a timely and user-accommodating manner.

In summary, what the business strategically demands of its I/T assets is cost-effective flexibility to enable dramatic maneuverability against a value chain background characterized by constantly shifting needs for information exchange between the value chain participants. CSC offers the means to make the I/T assets phenomenally responsive to diversity. The mission and challenge to the I/T organization then is to implement CSC so as to provide, in fact, the maximum flexibility at the minimum cost.

The original question we asked was, "How, if at all, does client/server computing contribute to I/T–business alignment?" The answer is straightforward: Client/server computing contributes to I/T business alignment by creating robust operational flexibility to profit from business environmental uncertainty and complexity. Regardless of the strategy triplet chosen, CSC offers the value proposition of operational flexibility to permit the business to cope with value chain fluctuations that keep moving toward a state bordering on entropy.

Another way to appreciate this most important point is to use an analogy from modern physics. In classical physics, the Newtonian laws of motion are completely deterministic. Given that the vector (direction and momentum) of an object and the forces acting upon it are known, what will transpire is completely calculable. Newtonian motion is subject to laws of causality and is comfortably predictable to the knowledgeable observer. In modern quantum physics, the domain of subnuclear particles, Newtonian determinism and causality has been replaced by probability. What motion will happen is subject to chance and can best be described as probabilistic. Causality has become uncomfortably random. A similar shift has happened to business. In previous decades, business actions were deterministic and I/T requirements and demands were predictable. This is no longer the case. The business environment, as was illustrated by the environmental diversity value chain, has become nondeterministic. What will be done, what will work, when it will be done, etc. has become probabilistic. To align means to align with uncertainty and randomness. An I/T architecture is required that can cope with this abruptness of the business playing field and that architecture is client/server.

THE MPS AND PSCS REVISITED

Now that we have a sharper understanding of the strategic positioning of client/server computing, we can began our initial rebuttal of the assertions of both the MPS and the PSCS. If we turn our attention first to the PSCS and reconsider Figure 2.17, the shallowness and nearsightedness of the PSCS position is blatant. Proprietary I/T products certainly can suboptimize specific islands of information movement and management. But as we have discovered, that is not the problem and, au contraire, is a contributor to the root cause of the problem. When you suboptimize, in the way that the PSCS would advise, you choose, by designs of your own making, to limit the dynamic reconfigurability of your I/T assets to deal with the constantly shifting value chain. Yes, for a moment the highly customized and proprietary solution is optimal, but what happens the next day when new customers or different suppliers who do not adhere to your provincial view need to be collaborated with? What happens when the strategy triplet is revised and suddenly the domain of sharing has to be extended beyond your comfortable shell? The reality is that proprietary solutions are arguments in favor of tactical solutions that solve an immediate problem at the far greater expense of constricting the strategic freedom of the business to compete through electronic relationships. If you follow the logic of our PSCS colleagues, you will inevitably trap yourself: You will become an I/T isolationist. Proprietary solutions do not provide the necessary operational flexibility to cope with the reality of marketplace competition in the next millennium.

In actuality, the promotion of proprietary interfaces, products, and solutions is characteristic of the earliest stage of an engineering discipline. All engineering disciplines go through three stages on their way to maturity:

1. *Craft Stage:* This stage is characterized by the development of solutions based on intuition and brute force by virtuosos and artisans.
2. *Commercial Stage:* This stage is characterized by the development of solutions by skilled journeymen through training, repeatable procedures, and apprenticeship/mentoring.
3. *Engineering Discipline:* This stage is characterized by the development of solutions by professionals in a shared community of expertise based on scientific theory and standard practices.

If you investigate mature engineering disciplines like mechanical engineering, electronic engineering, civil engineering, and so on, all of which have reached the engineering discipline stage, you will discover that standards are prevalent. For some reason, the PSCS believes that software and systems development should remain stalled forever in the craft stage. The imposition of standards with predictable functionality that promote interoperability, portability, scalability, reconfigurability, and so on is symptomatic of engineering progress and is to be welcomed. All the other engineering disciplines manage to innovate and be entrepreneurial with the "burden" of standards.

There is no advantage to keeping I/T padlocked in the dark ages. A hundred years from now, when people look back at the history of I/T, of all the debates that occurred, the question of standards will be viewed as the one most demonstrating the primitive stage of I/T maturity during our era. The promotion of proprietary solutions not only shows a lack of strategic acumen, it demonstrates a commitment to engineering primitivism.

Figure 2.17 also provides the basis for understanding the incoherence of the MPS assertions. As we have argued, the way to cope with escalating business environmental diversity is through robust flexibility. It is through malleability, adaptability, and agility of response that a business can successfully navigate the constantly shifting value chain environment. What the MPS would have us believe is that such a capability is a "trendy intangible." What the MPS would have us believe is that monolithic host-based computing, a single architecture from a single vendor (Figure 1.10), offers sufficient flexibility. Conversely, they would have us believe that the 32 varieties of CSC (Figure 1.9) are not needed. In other words, what they would have us believe is that the narrow and the solid is better for coping with diversity than the broad and the amorphous.

If you would recall from our earlier discussion on the nature of flexibility, an I/T architecture, A_1, is more flexible then another architecture, B_1, if the set of possible architectural choices available following architecture A_1 includes the set of possible architectural choices following architecture B_1. With CSC, through proper partitioning of the software layers as presented in Figure 1.9, all the layers can run on one processor in a monolithic architecture. However, since they were designed to work within a client/server architecture, they can be deployed in any of the other 35 configurations, if and when desired. This is the very essence of flexibility, and it sits at the heart of CSC. Why, as our MPS colleagues would suggest, are you better off confined to one and only one architectural solution when you can have a solution that includes that solution but many others as well?

While both the MPS and PSCS chastise CSC as being prohibitively expensive, cost must be first understood and analyzed within the context of meeting a user's needs. A car that is cheap but does not run is prodigal at any price. An architecture that is fixed and immobile is exceedingly dear at any price. The business environmental diversity demand on I/T architecture is for an architecture that can go through a continuing state of metamorphosis. This is something that CSC can do and something that monolithic computing cannot do. While we will expand this argument in the next two chapters, the truth is that even if host-based computing were cheaper than CSC (we will contest that in Chapter 4), the value proposition that it offers is insufficient at any price. An I/T architecture that prepositions you to lose is too expensive even if it were free.

In summary, our first refutation to the MPS and PSCS is as follows:

- Standards are necessary to cope with business environmental diversity. They are a critical enabler of movement.
- Standards are characteristic of a mature (science-based) engineering discipline. Proprietary systems are symptomatic of a primitive engineering discipline.
- Flexibility is the primary mechanism to cope with diversity. Client/server architecture is a robust architecture that supports a wide variety of configurations including host-based. Why settle for being a solid when you can be solid when you wish to be and be a changeling when you need to be?
- I/T architecture cost must be debated within the context of its value proposition. Monolithic host-centered computing and CSC are not simple commodity substitutes for each other. CSC offers a much superior value proposition based on its architectural variety, which aligns it with business needs. CSC delivers to business management the precious gift of options.

Strategic misalignment between the business and I/T has been a chronic condition for 15 years. CSC is a means to alleviating it. CSC is always the best architectural structure for I/T regardless of the triplet strategy. The MPS/PSCs are wrong in their assertions.

SUMMARY

The intent of this chapter was to answer critical questions regarding aligning I/T with business strategy. Our conclusions are as follows:

- Corporate strategy may be modeled as a data point between a pure union strategy and a pure multistate strategy.
- SBU strategy, with the corporate strategy influence, can be modeled as a data point between a pure union and a pure multistate strategy.
- An I/T centralized, dispersed, or integrated governance structure for both development and operations must be overlaid on the corporate strategy/SBU strategy pair.

- I/T must function within a hypermutating business environment. Since the environment is so variegated and unstable, it is obvious that the only way to cope with variety is with greater variety. This leads to the crucial strategic insight that I/T must first be managed for adaptability and then for economies:[6]
- Client/Server is always the preferred I/T architecture regardless of the (corporate strategy, SBU strategy, I/T structure) triplet.
- The ideas of the MPS and PSCS are incompatible with strategic alignment.

So what must be done is obvious; we must redesign the I/T organization to put it into a state of perfect alignment. The four steps to alignment are as follows:

1. Understand and model corporate strategy.
2. Understand and model SBU strategy.
3. Position I/T development and operations to strategically align with the corporate strategy/SBU strategy pair.
4. Reengineer the resulting I/T organizations around a client/server architecture as the coping mechanism for environmental diversity.

The I/T organization must be aligned, it must be cost effective, and it must be able to change quicker than the business.

EPILOGUE

One of the most instructive aphorisms from *The Art of War* is

> Go forth where they do not expect it.
> Attack where they are unprepared.

These 13 words encapsulate the fundamental rule for victory. To win, you must be able to aggressively maneuver. To win, you must be able to surprise the marketplace. How will you ever do this if you are in a perpetual state of misalignment? How will you ever do this if your I/T architecture freezes you into frosty block of ice?

NOTES

1. Sun Tzu said, "Strategy is a problem of coordination, not of masses."

2. Development and operations could further be divided into "core" and "noncore" to facilitate surgical structuring. *Core* refers to applications and their production operations that support the business processes that provide competitive advantage to an SBU or the corporation. *Noncore* refers to the remaining business applications. We could further subdivide these items into class of application (transaction processing, decision support, or information sharing) and domain of application (personal, group, departmental, cross departmental, and enterprise). To maintain simplicity, we will not make these distinctions in the analysis.

3. We refer to this as a strategy triplet.

4. In strategic parlance, client/server computing solves what is known as the "consumer's dilemma." With many products or services, there are often key customer satisfiers that are at odds with each other. If the customer wants exceptional service, she will have to pay a premium price. Conversely, if she will settle for minimum service, she can get a product at a lower cost. The consumer's dilemma is the desire for exceptional service at a low cost. Normally, the consumer will have to settle for one or the other or some intermediate solution. Vendors excite customers by resolving the relevant consumer's dilemma. When suppliers can deliver a product that can address what were previously incompatible satisfiers, customers swarm to them.

This is exactly what is occurring with CSC. The consumer's dilemma in this instance is cost and flexibility. Client/server computing permits the consumer to have both and, consequently, client/server computing is an excitement product, a product that resolves the dilemma in a manner favorable to the customer's complete desires.

5. The Star Trek show, "Deep Space Nine," provides an interesting metaphor for the challenge of I/T architecture. During one episode, the character Odo, who is referred to as a "shape shifter," returns to his home planet. A shape shifter is a humanoid who can alter his shape at will; he is formless. At his native planet, they discuss the differences between themselves, who are actually a species called "changelings" and the other people of the galaxies whom they refer to as the "solids"—humanoids of a fixed and constant

form. In this elegant but simple allusion is compacted the entire issue of I/T architecture: the question of whether you will be a solid or a changeling. Will your business confront expanding environmental business diversity with an architecture that is a solid (monolithic host-based computing) or an architecture that is a changeling (client/server computing)?

6. A recent study by IBM Worldwide Client/Server Computing confirms this view. The top four objectives in moving to CSC were

Flexibility to respond to business changes.

Better customer service.

Increased employee productivity.

Multiuser access to information.

Lowering operational costs was fifth.

3

Understanding Client/Server Computing Strategically

When I reexamine the arguments of the MPS (see Chapter 1 and Appendix A), two glaring assertions repeatedly capture my attention: "No one really understands the reasons for moving off the mainframe," and "We are moving off the mainframe but do not know why."

Apparently, neither their own efforts nor the labor of others has been able to satisfactorily explain to them the strategic logic of client/server computing. The industry migration to client/server computing remains to them an enigmatic mystery. In this chapter, we try to alleviate this problem. Perhaps once the logic of CSC is adequately explained, they will join the migration with enthusiasm rather than remain saddled with specious reasoning. The reason for migrating to client/server computing is not arcane; it is strategic advantage.

Several arguments combine to explain the logic of "why we are moving off the mainframe." It is the totality of the arguments that explains the advantages and superiority of CSC and, while these must be explained and grasped individually, they should be reflected upon in unison. The first argument was presented in Chapter 2, where we argued that the fundamental problem of I/T–business alignment is the overlaying of a flexible and cost-effective I/T architecture on the shifting environmental diversity that characterizes modern business. This permits business processes to be continually revised in accord with dynamic business times and circumstances. By virtue of its fluid architecture, CSC provides a more ideal solution to this problem than monolithic host-based computing. Why be limited to one fixed architectural solution when you can have 36 that include that one?

In Chapter 4, we provide our final argument in favor of CSC, which is that, contrary to the repeated claims of the MPS and PSCS, CSC will prove to be a much cheaper architecture than host-based computing. The cost argument is unquestionably the most damaging argument against CSC and must be refuted individually. Since most I/T management teams are fanatically cost obsessed, raising fears of high costs is a very effective FUD technique to throttle migration.

In this chapter, we present five linked arguments that provide the heart of the refutation to the MPS and CSPS pair:

1. *Value Positioning:* This argument compares host-based computing and client/server computing in terms of their competing value propositions.
2. *Maneuver:* This argument compares CSC and host-based computing in terms of their abilities to support an attrition or maneuver style of business competition.
3. *S Curve Analysis:* This argument uses S curve analysis, the primary tool for analyzing technology substitution and diffusion, to explain the specious reasoning of many of the MPS assertions. To understand the inevitability of the replacement of mainframe computing by client/server, we must appreciate the nonspecific mechanics of technological substitution and market diffusion theory and how the problem at hand is but an instance of such.
4. *Strategic Paradox:* This argument explains why the obvious linear logic that supports mainframe computing is spurious and shows that the strategic framework of strategic paradox explains why, if I/T is to be used strategically, CSC is the right architecture.
5. *Vision:* This argument compares the strategic visions of the two competing approaches.

In this way, proponents of CSC should be reassured, encouraged, and reinvigorated in their efforts, and MPS members should no longer wander about aimlessly wondering "why?"

VALUE POSITIONING

By virtue of being consumers in a free market economy, all of us are quite familiar and skilled, in practice if not in theory, with the notions of a value line, a product price, a value proposition, and a value point. Figure 3.1 illustrates a value line. The following ideas are communicated by it:

- A product is sold at a price and offers some value proposition to the consumer at that price. The value proposition defines all the attributes of the product (i.e., feature/functionality, service, warranty, support, image, packaging, etc). The intersection of a price with a value proposition is called a value point. When a consumer makes a purchase decision, she votes with her dollars that for that price, the associated value proposition is worth what she paid for it.
- There are many products offered to a market at varying paired prices and value propositions. The value points for these products form a value line. The value line has the interesting characteristic that while prices and value propositions will vary widely, the ratios of price to value proposition, the value line ratio, along the value line will remain nearly constant; that is, for a given value line, P_1(price)/P_1(value proposition) = P_2(price)/P_2(value proposition) = P_3(price)/P_3(value proposi-

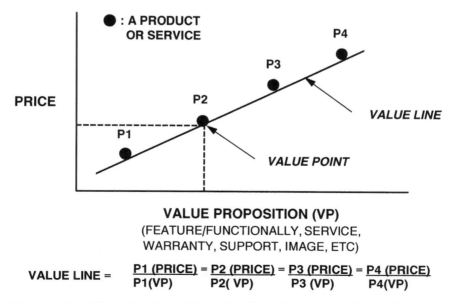

$$\text{VALUE LINE} = \frac{\text{P1 (PRICE)}}{\text{P1(VP)}} = \frac{\text{P2 (PRICE)}}{\text{P2(VP)}} = \frac{\text{P3 (PRICE)}}{\text{P3 (VP)}} = \frac{\text{P4 (PRICE)}}{\text{P4(VP)}}$$

Figure 3.1   The value line. The value line shows the relationship between competing products' price and value propositions.

tion) $= P_n$(price)$/P_n$(value proposition). In this way, there is value in linear proportion to cost.

- Consider what happens in a free market if the value line ratio does not remain linearly proportional. As shown in Figure 3.2, if the price is held constant and products are offered at value proposition points P_{1a} and P_{1b} relative to P_1, it is immediately obvious that P_{1a} is a bad value and P_{1b} is a good value. As consumers learn about product P_{1b}, it will win ever-greater market share. Why buy P_{1a} when for the same money you can get a better value package with P_{1b}? The competing vendors will therefore form a new value line around P_{1b}, or, as market awareness spreads, they will all go out of business. Now consider, as shown in Figure 3.3, what happens if the value proposition is held constant but products are offered at various prices. If the value proposition is held constant and products are offered at price points P_{1a} and P_{1b} relative to P_1, it is immediately obvious that P_{1a} is overpriced and P_{1b} is a bargain. As consumers learn about product P_{1b}, it will win ever-greater market share. Why buy P_{1a} when you can get the same value proposition at a lower cost with P_{1b}? The competing vendors will therefore form a new value line around P_{1b} or, again, as market awareness spreads, they will go out of business.

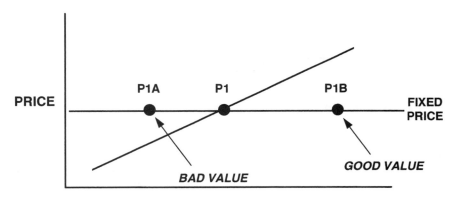

Figure 3.2   Good value/bad value. If you fix the price, products priced to the left and right of the value line offer a bad value and good value, respectively.

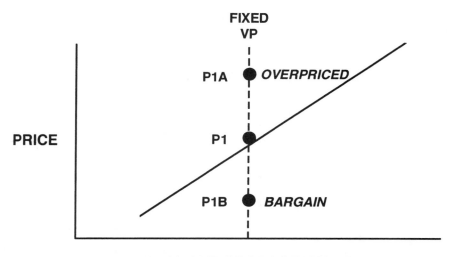

Figure 3.3 Bargain and overpriced. If you hold the value proposition fixed, products above and below the value line are overpriced and a bargain, respectively.

One way of understanding competition, then, is the struggle to offer an ever more attractive moving value point to your market than your competitors can. Understanding and comparing products, then, requires not merely discussing costs but discussing value propositions as well.

If we use the value line framework, we can insightfully understand the MPS and CSPS arguments as asserting that CSC is the worst of both worlds (i.e., as shown in Figure 3.4, CSC is both overpriced and a bad value). It is not surprising, therefore, that they feel that I/T management has been swindled and bamboozled. The self-serving vendors and consultants have not only gotten the I/T executives to overpay, they have gotten them to pay a premium for an inferior product. I, of course, believe that the real situation is exactly the opposite and, as shown in Figure 3.5, CSC offers an exceptional value proposition at a superior price. I/T management has not been deceived but has shown exceptional strategic acumen in intuitively understanding the superior value point of CSC.

We will argue the cost issue in Chapter 4. What we wish to focus

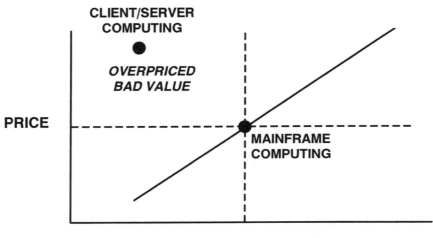

Figure 3.4   **The MPS assertion. The MPS and CSPS assert that CSC is both overpriced and a bad value proposition relative to mainframe computing.**

on now is the value proposition issue. Simply put, most of the interesting technologies that enable meaningful reengineering of a business in exciting ways to engage in advantageous relationships with the value chain partners are client/server based. Work-flow technologies, multimedia, graphical user interfaces (GUIs), and future user interfaces such as sight, speech, and virtual reality, groupware, pen-based computing, e-mail, video conferencing, object oriented in all its myriad of forms, distributed transaction management, and distributed database are all client/server based. Similarly, the architectural characteristics that provide value in dealing with the business environmental diversity (i.e., interoperability, portability, scalability, modularity, vendor neutrality, and reconfigurability) are client/server based. The truth is, a reengineering discussion centered around using monolithic host-based computing offerings is a very short meeting. More important, however, is the stark truth that mainframe computing has been a dismal strategic failure (i.e., it has offered little, if any, strategic value to the business) while CSC offers dramatic therapy.

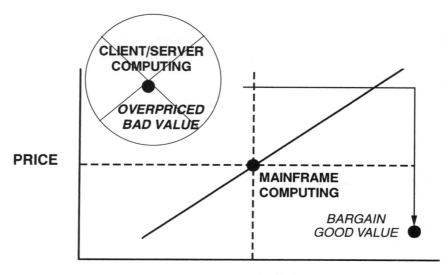

VALUE PROPOSITION (VP)
(FEATURE/FUNCTIONALLY, SERVICE,
WARRANTY, SUPPORT, IMAGE, ETC.)

Figure 3.5   **The CSC assertion. The CSPLA asserts that CSC not only offers a better value proposition than mainframe computing, it is also cheaper.**

Figures 3.6 through 3.11 offer studies from around the world, since 1988, on the key strategic issues facing I/T management. Figure 3.12 shows a similar study dating back to 1980. What is absolutely mind-boggling about these studies is the following:

- The strategic issues across countries are relatively constant. The inability to use I/T strategically is happening globally.
- These issues barely ever change. In spite of thousands of corporate years of effort in addressing these problems, they remain intractable. The turnover rate is actually slowing, with fewer issues leaving and previous issues returning.
- The strategic issues that confronted I/T executives in 1980 are, in large part, the same issues that confront I/T management in 1995.
- There is little, if any, strategic progress. Like the mythical figure Sisyphus who was condemned to push a rock up a hill for eternity just to have it fall to the bottom again when he

Issue	'94	'93	'92	'91	'90	'89	'88
Business Reengineering Through I/T	1	1	2	1	1	11	N/R
Aligning I/S with Business Goals	2	2	1	2	4	2	1
Utilizing Data	3	4	4	5	7	6	7
Cross-Functional Information Systems	4	4	6	3	3	7	N/R
Information Architecture	5	7	3	8	9	5	5
Systems Development	6	3	9	4	6	13	12
Updating Obsolete Systems	7	8	18	N/R	13	N/R	18
Integrating Systems	8	11	13	9	16	12	6
Improving the I/S Human Resource	9	12	5	13	11	8	8
Changing Technology Platform	9	10	N/R	N/R	N/R	N/R	N/R
I/S Strategic Plan	11	9	10	6	5	4	2
Cutting I/S Costs	12	6	11	11	10	14	17
Capitalizing on I/T Advances	13	14	19	20	N/R	17	N/R
Managing Dispersed Systems	14	12	15	19	N/R	16	13
Using I/T for Competitive Breakthroughs	15	15	14	12	8	14	
Connecting to Customers/Suppliers	16	16	20	15	19	N/R	N/R
Moving to Open Systems	17	19	N/R	N/R	N/R	N/R	N/R
Educating Management on I/T	18	18	16	14	2	3	3
Promoting I/S Function	19	20	17	17	15	N/R	N/R
Improving Leadership Skills	20	17	7	10	N/R	N/R	N/R

Figure 3.6   I/T strategic issues: 1988–1994 North America. This study documents the top 20 strategic issues for the past seven years in North America. (Source: *CSC/Index*.)

reached the top, I/T executives perpetually are confronted with the same intractable strategic problems.

• Corporate leadership is asked each year, year after year, to fund strategic initiatives for the same set of problems. Would any other area of the business request funding for the exact same list of problems year after year and get away with it?

In spite of the self-comforting accolades that our MPS friends routinely assert on the meritorious service of mainframe comput-

Issue	'94	'93	'92	'91	'90	'89	'88
Business Reengineering Through I/T	1	1	19	2	1	17	N/R
Cutting I/S Costs	2	2	8	9	11	16	16
Aligning I/S and Corporate Goals	3	3	1	4	2	3	2
Cross-Functional Information Systems	4	4	9	7	3	5	N/R
Utilizing Data	5	7	4	17	4	7	12
Systems Development	6	11	18	5	9	10	14
Information Architecture	7	4	5	12	6	8	5
Improving the I/S Human Resource	8	6	3	6	10	4	7
Managing Dispersed Systems	9	14	14	N/R	N/R	N/R	N/R
Promoting I/S Function	9	N/R	N/R	N/R	N/R	N/R	N/R
Educating Management on I/T	11	14	12	20	18	N/R	19
Updating Obsolete Systems	12	12	16	13	10	14	17
Integrating Systems	13	7	12	10	14	14	10
Changing Technology Platform	14	9	N/R	N/R	N/R	N/R	N/R
Moving to Open Systems	15	9	N/R	N/R	N/R	N/R	N/R
Using I/T for Competitive Breakthroughs	16	N/R	11	1	7	1	4
I/S Strategic Plan	17	12	2	3	5	2	1
Managing I/T Changes	17	17	N/R	N/R	12	9	8
Connecting to Customers/Suppliers	19	16	N/R	14	8	N/R	N/R
Determining the Value of I/T	20	N/R	20	N/R	17	19	N/R

Figure 3.7   **I/T strategic issues: 1988–1994 Europe. This study documents the top 20 strategic issues for the past seven years in Europe. (Source: *CSC/Index*.)**

ing, the truth is that during the mainframe watch, over the last 15 years, it has not been possible to:

- Achieve alignment of I/T with business strategy.
- Build cross-functional systems.
- Implement an I/T architecture.
- Provide broad access to data.
- Control development costs.
- Improve the speed and quality of development.
- Develop a strategic I/T plan.

Issue	'88
Cutting I/S Costs	1
Currency with I/T Change	2
Connectivity and Networking	3
Improving the I/S Human Resource	4
Aligning I/S and Corporate Goals	5
User Satisfaction	6
Changing Technology Platform	7
Data Security	8
Moving to Open Systems	9
Educating Management on I/T	10

Figure 3.8   **I/T strategic issues: 1988 Australia. This study documents the top 10 strategic issues in Australia. (Source: *Australian Computer Journal*.)**

What we have been able to achieve, however, is a situation where we are about to confront the need to navigate the business environmental diversity value chain (Figure 2.17) burdened with massive mainframe system obsolescence. The real unspoken truth is that while mainframe computing has been reasonably successful

Issue	'92
I/S Strategic Plan	1
Improving the I/S Human Resource	2
Information Architecture	3
Systems Development	4
Aligning I/S and Corporate Goals	5
Promoting I/S Function	6
Using I/T for Competitive Breakthroughs	7
Managing Dispersed Systems	8
Data Utilization	9
Educating Management on I/T	10

Figure 3.9   **I/T strategic issues: 1992 Canada. This study documents the top 10 strategic issues in Canada. (Source: Canada Datasystems.)**

Issue	'92
Promoting I/S Function	1
Improving the I/S Human Resource	2
Quality of Data	3
Educating Management on I/T	4
User Friendliness	5
Improving the I/S Human Resource	6
Software Maintenance	7
Standards	8
Data Security	9
Packaged Software	10
Culture Barriers	10
Hardware Maintenance	12
Aligning I/S and Corporate Goals	13
Data Utilization	14
Productivity	15
Applications Portfolio	16
Computer Hardware	17
I/S Strategic Plan	18
Political Climate	19
Connectivity	20

Figure 3.10   **I/T strategic issues: 1992 India. This study documents the top 20 strategic issues in India. (Source: International Information Systems.)**

in automating mundane business processes, it has been a strategic disaster.

To clarify, the problem is not that there are strategic issues. There will always be new opportunities, challenges, and problems that need to be addressed. The problem is that for a set of issues defined in 1980, little to no progress has been made. They are unquestionably important issues that we would expect to see on such a list. Even more important, they should have been addressed. Strategic issues are not issues that cannot be solved; they are issues that must be solved for the well-being of the business. Outsourcing as a solution to I/T management is not surprising when you look at the strategic I/T report card in this light.

Issue	'94
User Communications	1
Educating Management on I/T	2
I/S Strategic Plan	3
Using I/T for Competitive Breakthroughs	4
Aligning I/S with Business Goals	5
Computerization of Routine Work	6
Information Architecture	7
Integrating Systems	8
Development Productivity	9
System Friendliness	10
Security	11
Development Quality	12
Standards	12
Utilizing Data	14
I/S Funding	15
Promoting I/S Function	16
User Participation	17
Improving the I/S Human Resource	18
Information Architecture	19
Placement of I/T Department	20

Figure 3.11   **I/T strategic issues: 1994 Republic of China. This study documents the top 20 strategic issues in the Republic of China. (Source: *Information and Management*.)**

There is a tremendous paradox at play here. On one hand, we have proponents of mainframe computing telling us we should recentralize I/T because of how successful mainframe computing is and will continue to be. On the other hand, we have seven global studies showing no strategic progress in the use of I/T since 1980. Assuming companies have been diligently working on these issues, why are they intractable with regard to mainframe computing? I will propose an answer later in this chapter when we discuss strategic paradox.

Issue	1987	1986	1984	1983	1982	1980
Strategic Planning	1	1	1	1	1	1
Competitive Advantage	2	2	N/R	N/R	N/R	N/R
Organizational Learning	3	3	6	6	N/R	8
I/S Role and Contribution	4	4	N/R	N/R	N/R	N/R
Alignment	5	5	7	7	N/R	9
End-User Computing	6	6	2	2	N/R	10
Data as Resource	7	7	9	9	N/R	4
Information Architecture	8	8	N/R	N/R	N/R	N/R
Measuring I/S Effectiveness	9	9	5	5	2	2
Integrating DP, OA, and FA	10	10	3	3	6	N/R
Software Development			4	4	N/R	6
I/T Human Resource			8	8	7	7
DSS Systems			10	10	5	5
Telecommunications					3	3
Role of I/T Manager					4	N/R
Educating Management					8	N/R
I/S Centralization/ Decentralization					9	N/R
Employee Job Satisfaction					10	N/R

Figure 3.12 **I/T strategic issues: 1980–1987 North America. This study documents the top 10 strategic issues in North America from 1980 to 1987. (Source: *MIS Quarterly*.)**

A strong case can be made that CSC addresses most of the issues that have remained obstinate over these last 15 years. As shown in Table 3.1, CSC offers direct or adjunct theory for 15 issues.[1] That is more than amazing, it is almost miraculous that one technology could offer so much therapy for so many persistent problems. Why this is such is discussed later in our section on strategic paradox.

The real value positioning of CSC and mainframe computing is shown in Figure 3.13. Mainframe computing offers fundamentally bad value because it offers no strategic value. Client/server, by virtue of its changeling characteristics, offers tremendous strategic value. While the cost issue will be resolved in the next chapter, let

Table 3.1
CSC Therapy.

1994 Strategic I/T Issue	Client/Server Computing Therapy
1. Business reengineering through I/T	CSC provides a robust architecture to reengineer upon.
2. Aligning corporate and information systems goals	CSC permits improved access to data, sharing of resources, modular adoption of new technologies, and navigation of the environmental diverse value chain.
3. Utilizing data	CSC provides a decoupled architecture that permits broad access to both subject databases that are used to run the business and decision support databases that are used to analyze the business.
4. Instituting cross-functional systems	CSC provides the required architecture to permit sharing of I/T processing and data resources.
5. Creating an information architecture	Client/Server provides the heart of a robust processing architecture that enables reach, range, and maneuverability for the business.
6. Improving systems development	The C/S attributes of adaptability, flexibility, modularity, data accessibility, and so on all improve the enterprise's ability to rapidly deliver software by reuse rather than new development.
7. Updating obsolescent systems	C/S can be appended in various configurations to existing systems and thereby permit graduated renovation.
8. Integrating systems	Interoperability is at the heart of CSC.
9. Changing technology platforms	CSC provides the basis for a software-centric architecture that will permit migration across evolving hardware platforms,
10. Cutting I/S costs	CSC will provide I/T savings through the downward cost curves of basic C/S technologies and massive reuse through architecture.
11. Capitalizing on I/T advances	CSC is an open software architecture that, by design, welcomes changes.

Table 3.1
(Continued)

1994 Strategic I/T Issue	Client/Server Computing Therapy
12. Managing dispersed systems	CSC architecture provides the foundation architecture to mange C/S systems as well as run them.
13. Using I/T for competitive advantage	Advantage is built by overlaying I/T flexibility over the business environmental diversity. The required I/T flexibility is provided by CSC.
14. Connecting to customers and suppliers	CSC is a relationship-building architecture.
15. Moving to open systems	CSC is built upon open systems.

CSC provides direct therapy for most of the major 1994 strategic I/T issues.

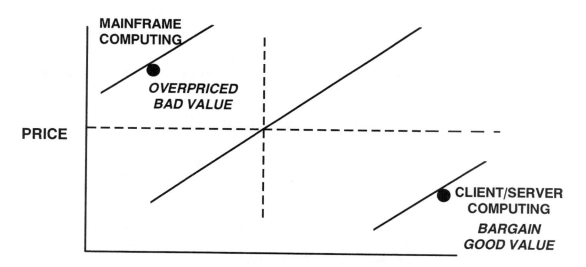

Figure 3.13 **Real value positioning. CSC offers a far superior value proposition than mainframe computing.**

us assume for the moment that CSC is more expensive. Even so, does not the improved value ratio more than compensate? After 15 years of strategic failure with mainframe computing, do you believe the next 15 will be any better? The simple truth is that mainframe computing is satisfactory for performing mundane administrative applications but lacks the attributes to be the spearhead of strategic computing. This client/server can do, and the logic of that will be explained when we discuss strategic paradox.

With this understanding of value propositions as they relate to mainframe computing and CSC, imagine a situation where mainframe computing was free and CSC continued to cost money. We grant to the MPS the maximum advantage. I would suggest that companies would still move to CSC. They would move to CSC because what good is something, even if free, if it doesn't deliver the required value proposition to compete. Companies with free mainframe computing will be unable to cope with the value chain diversity (Figure 2.17). Their cost advantage with free I/T will be short-lived when they are unable to maneuver against the improved relationships developed by their CSC-based competitors. They will be very efficient at delivering what people wanted but no longer want.

The summary of the value positioning argument is as follows:

- Price (or cost) is only meaningful in the context of the value proposition received.
- While the MPS would have us believe that mainframes have offered an outstanding value proposition and the CSPS would have us believe that proprietary systems have provided us with tremendous value, the strategic truth is just the opposite. Even a casual review of the research on strategic issues of I/T shows that little to no progress has been made during the mainframe watch.
- The reason for the mainframe's strategic failure is actually easy to explain and is explained in the discussion of strategic paradox later in this chapter.
- Client/server computing offers strategic therapy for most of the outstanding strategic issues. This is because the CSC changeling attributes, which mainframe computing lacks, are critical in solving these issues.
- It is therefore meaningless to compare mainframe costs to CSC costs without regard to their competing value proposi-

tions. CSC's value proposition is far to the right of mainframe computing, and there is no way for mainframe computing to move to match it. It cannot move because it is a solid. While CSC and mainframe computing are substitutes for each other, they are not commodity substitutes.

Sun Tzu taught that to win, you must contest your opponents strategically. The best strategy always is to use strategy to ruin your opponent's strategy and thereby cause the adversary to submit with the absolute minimum expenditure of effort. How will that be done with an architecture, host-based computing, that has such a dismal strategic legacy? To the contrary, CSC will offer management unparalleled options.

MANEUVER

Businesses must always be prepared to respond creatively to marketplace dynamics. The normal marketplace state is constant upheaval. It is therefore obvious that those companies that can navigate with greater alacrity, speed, and dexterity have a distinct advantage. In fact, with speed, alacrity, and dexterity as your allies, you can further exaggerate your advantage by deliberately promoting marketplace dynamics to the benefit of your customers and the detriment of your competitors.

Companies take two basic approaches to engage the marketplace:

1. *Attrition Fighter:* Marketplace supremacy is achieved by taking a strong but fixed position and "slugging it out" for marketplace dominance. Through direct confrontational marketplace battles, by concentrating superior assets against inferior foes, you win by exhausting the opponent's will and ability to compete. The optimum situation is to win in a few decisive battles and, by virtue of your demonstrated superior power, deter other competitors from stepping into your marketplace and challenging you. An attrition fighter, like a classical heavyweight boxer, wins by superiority of assets and the ability to deliver a crushing and decisive knockout blow.

2. *Maneuver Fighter:* Marketplace superiority is achieved by staying in motion. A maneuver fighter continually looks for oppor-

tunistic gaps in the marketplace and swiftly moves her assets to that point to maximize her opportunity. The maneuver fighter attempts to continually disrupt the marketplace by changing the rules of competition. It is by the actions of movement that advantage is gained. Advantage is best understood as a succession of overlapping temporary advantages rather than a set of sustainable competitive advantages. The maneuver fighter expects that the maneuver process will cause friction and disruption in the ability of her opponents to respond. At best, this will eventually lead to a collapse in her opponent's business systems. A maneuver fighter is best illustrated in the dictum of the great heavyweight fighter Mohammed Ali who said, "Float like a butterfly, sting like a bee." A maneuver fighter uses speed, flexibility, opportunism, and dexterity to chip away at the edges of the marketplace until the entire marketplace has been challenged. In doing so, unlike the attrition fighter, a deliberate attempt is made to avoid expensive, time-consuming, and exhausting direct confrontations with competitors. You win by artfulness through indirection, not by force.[2]

When one reviews the last 15 years of global competition and the negative change in fortune of numerous former outstanding companies and the emergence of new successful companies, it would be safe to assert that there is a fundamental marketplace shift occurring from national wars of attrition to global wars of maneuver.

A company's marketplace style can be illustrated as shown in Figure 3.14. Though rarely articulated as such, most companies have a primary and secondary style with which they engage the marketplace. It is fashionable for gurus, academics, and consultants to tell clients that they must reengineer their business, they must renovate themselves, they must reinvent their value proposition, they must rediscover their culture, and they must redesign their business formula. I take this to mean that most companies have formally positioned themselves as "Big A's" (Figure 3.14) and, if they are to compete against the swift and the nimble, must migrate to one of the other cells. The 1990s forward is the era of the maneuver fighter, not the attrition fighter.

If companies, regardless of their former achievements, are to move to a maneuver market competitive style, what impact does this have on I/T? I assert that if the business moves from a style of being a fixed position fighter to being an always-in-motion maneu-

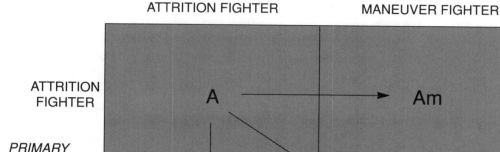

Figure 3.14 Marketplace style. Companies that were formerly attrition fighters are moving to a style that includes maneuver capabilities. (Source: *Practical Steps to Aligning Information Technology with Business Strategies,* Bernard H. Boar, John Wiley & Sons, Inc., 1994.)

ver fighter, it would seem reasonable to expect that the I/T assets will likewise have to be redesigned to support the new style. It would be extraordinarily fortuitous that an I/T style that supported an attrition style would also be ideal for a maneuver style. It would seem, to the contrary, that the attributes of I/T that you would prize would be exact opposites.

So even if we were to concede that mainframe computing has been an absolutely wonderful architecture, it was a wonderful architecture for yesterday's wars of attrition. However, it does not have the attributes to support wars of maneuver. In other words, as the business realigns itself to become a swift, agile, and flexible maneuver fighter and leaves its attrition character behind, I/T assets also have to shed their attrition legacy and move forward to new configurations that will enable maneuver marketplace encounters. I/T architecture, to maintain a state of strategic alignment with the business, must move from an attrition architecture, mainframe computing, to a maneuver architecture, client/server computing.

A rich framework to understand how I/T architecture should be formulated to support a business maneuver market style is called a reach, range, and maneuver architecture and is shown in Figure 3.15.[3] Client/server computing sits in the center of this architecture. Reach defines whom, from where, and when I/T resources may be reached. Ranges defines what I/T assets, data and services, can be reached. Maneuver defines the attributes of applications that are built on top of the reach and range that enable tremendous flexibility.

To support a maneuver business style, it is necessary to support business processes that will undergo continuous reconfiguration. As we saw before with Figure 2.17, it will be necessary to constantly reconfigure the I/T architecture to be able to cope with the expanding environmental business diversity. So the client/server attributes of modularity, scalability, adaptability, portability, openness, interoperability, data accessibility, and maintainability are all essential to both aligning with and coping with a business that will engage in a maneuver market style. As shown in Figure 3.16, the I/T architecture must become a shape shifter. It does this by having the applications inherit maneuverability attributes from the architecture rather than building them individually

Monolithic host-centered computing has no record of being able to cope with or support fast-paced maneuverability. To the contrary, the whole basis of mainframe advantage is in its fixed and predictable nature. The mainframe is a solid and, as such, is the weapon of choice for attrition fighters. The new battles, however, are wars of maneuver, and for these wars, CSC is the indispensable weaponry.

Figure 3.17 provides a final perspective on business strategy and maneuver. The idea of maneuver in a military context is to use mobility to shift or turn the front. In this way, not only do your forces not directly confront the enemy, but by virtue of maneuver, you leave all the supporting structures—command and control, logistics, and so on—misaligned. It is our assertion that businesses will also want to turn the front and that to do that rapidly they will need to be I/T architecture enabled. The architecture that will allow rapid turning of the marketplace fronts is a reach, range, and

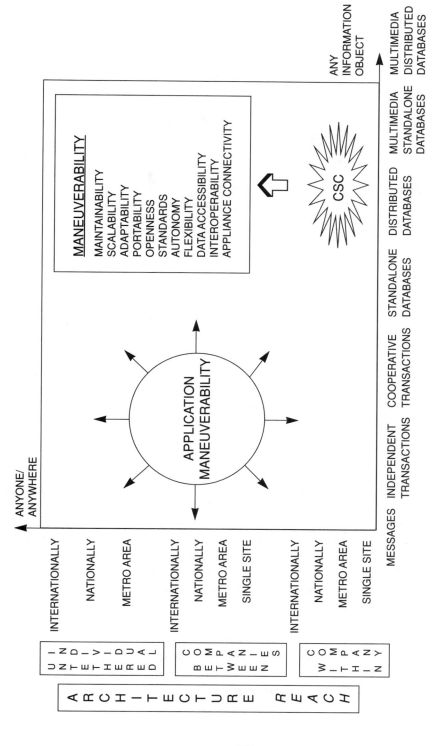

Figure 3.15 **Reach, range, and maneuverability architecture.** An I/T architecture achieves maximum benefits for a business when it achieves perfect reach, perfect range, and perfect maneuverability. (Source: *Implementing Client/Server Computing*, Bernard H. Boar, McGraw-Hill, 1993.)

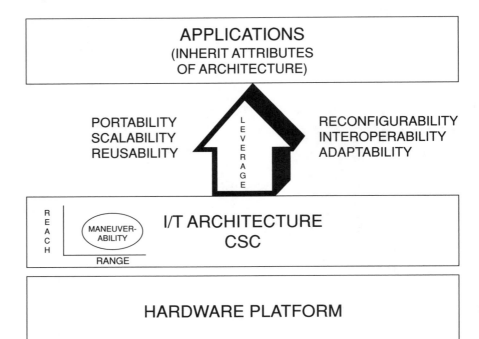

Figure 3.16   I/T as a shape shifter. I/T architecture must enable the business applications that run over it to undergo continuous metamorphosis.

maneuverable architecture that has CSC sitting at its center. This is another reason that I argued before that even if mainframe computing was free, companies will move to CSC. They will move to CSC because with monolithic host-centered computing they will not be able to maneuver; they will be fixed targets in a war of global movement.

To summarize the arguments in this section:

- Business competition is evolving from national wars of attrition to global wars of maneuver.
- Business demands with a nonnegotiable sense of urgency that I/T enable the business to fight in maneuver style—fast, nimble, and able to turn on a dime.

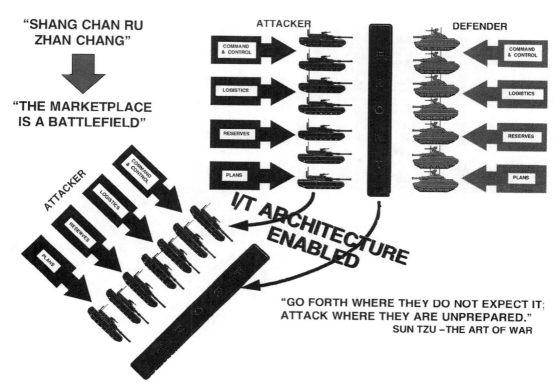

Figure 3.17 Maneuver is shifting/turning the front. The business requires that the I/T architecture enable it to turn the marketplace fronts.

- The means of response to these demands is a reach, range, and maneuverability architecture in which CSC sits at its center.
- Mainframe computing, regardless of its historical virtues, is an architecture of attrition, which is the wrong weaponry for a war of movement.

Figure 3.18 integrates the previous notion of business environmental diversity and the newly introduced notion of reach, range, and maneuverability. It is by overlaying the reach, range, and maneuver architecture on the value chain that the business is able to cope with the diversity and maneuver to create advantage.[4] It is by blanketing the environment with an I/T architecture that doesn't maintain any constant shape that you can win. Do you really believe that host-based computing can do this?

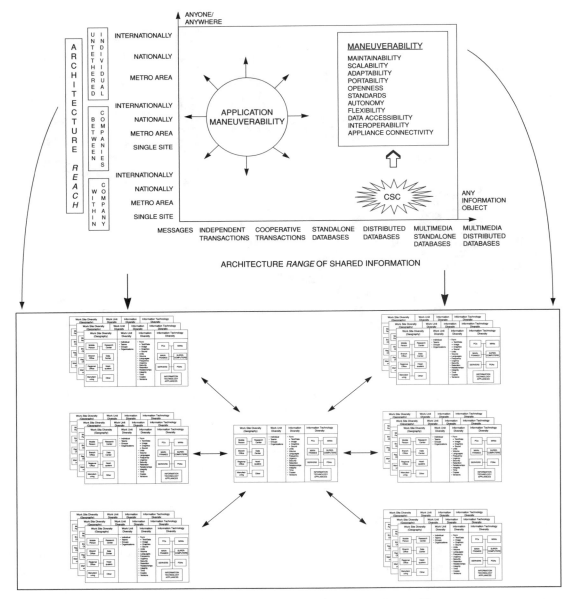

Figure 3.18   **Overlaying reach, range, and maneuverability on business environmental diversity. The way to cope with value chain diversity and enable dramatic adaptability is by blanketing the environment with a reach, range, and maneuverability architecture.**

S CURVE ANALYSIS

While the mainframe–CSC debate is very immediate and monumental to those of us in the I/T field who are touched by it on a daily basis, if you step back to observe the broader picture, you quickly discover that the mainframe–CSC duel is but one instance of the general and recurring phenomenon of *technological substitution and diffusion.* Technological substitution is the process by which one technology displaces another technology in performing a function or set of functions for a market. The substitute technology offers the customer an inducement to switch by virtue of an improved value point. Diffusion is the process by which a marketplace is educated about a substitute technology. So substitution is the process by which one technology challenges and replaces another and diffusion is the process through which the substitute is accepted or rejected by the marketplace.[5] Substitution and diffusion are the engines and instruments of economic progress; the great mainframe–CSC debate is, in reality, but another instance of this well-studied phenomenon.[6]

Technological substitution is underwritten by the perspective that people have an enduring set of basic needs. The pursuit of substitution is to find ever-better solutions (value propositions) for those relatively fixed needs. There are five basic drivers for new technologies:

1. *Serendipity:* An accidental discovery leads to the discovery of a superior technology.
2. *Military Research:* Military research and development leads to the discovery of a new commercial technology.
3. *Planned Obsolescence:* Commercial research and development is done to obsolete an existing product to renew market sales.
4. *Depletion of Resources:* The foreseeable depletion of some factor of production leads to research to develop a superior replacement before the resource is depleted.
5. *Competition:* The necessity of endlessly offering superior value propositions to customers stimulates intense research and development.

The last one, competitive pressures, is the one that impels the subject at hand.

Market diffusion is the dynamics of market acceptance of the substitution of a new product for an existing product. In technological diffusion and substitution jargon, the incumbent product is referred to as the *defender* and the substitute product is referred to as the *attacker*.[7] The speed of diffusion is a function of

- *Value Proposition:* How superior is the value proposition of the attacker to the defender?
- *Infrastructure:* How much infrastructure support must be put in place to support the new product?
- *Learning:* What communication channels are used to reach, persuade, and influence the market?
- *Ease of Substitution:* How much effort (time, cost, training, etc.) is required to adopt the attacker?
- *Defense:* How does the defender defend itself and, in doing so, alter the comparative value propositions?

Diffusion is usually expressed in terms of market share.

A product is understood to be a set of functions built on a technology asset base that meets some customer needs (see Figure 3.19). There are therefore three types of generic technological substitutions that may occur:

1. *Functional Substitution:* The attacker displaces the defender in performing some functions but not all. The attacker may also add new functions as well as replace existing functions. The relationship between the two products becomes complementary.
2. *Product Substitution:* The functionality of the defender is replaced in its entirety by the attacker. The defender's asset base remains viable, however.
3. *Asset Substitution:* Not only does the attacker replace the product, but it is done with a different set of technological assets that make obsolete and destroy the technology competencies and investments of the defender.

Figure 3.20 shows the three points of attack. A substitution attack is not necessarily constant in its target and, depending on situational dynamics, can swing between types.

The life cycle of a technology is routinely illustrated through the use of S curves[8] (Figure 3.21). The substitution process of two technologies is illustrated using dueling S curves (Figure 3.22). The basic logic of an S curve is as follows:

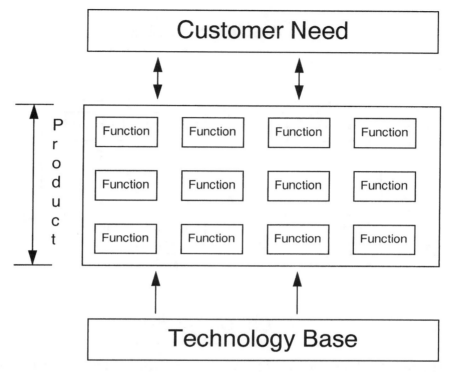

Figure 3.19   **A product. A product should be understood as a set of functions built on a technology base that meets a customer need.**

- All technologies should/must be understood in terms of performance limits. As investments are made in a technology, its price/performance improvement will follow an S curve shape (Figure 3.21).
- At first, Stage 1, the product will be incomplete and expensive, and appeal only to a niche market with very specific objectives for using the product.
- In Stages 2 and 3, dramatic improvements are made in the product. For every dollar invested in improving the product, there is a significantly greater return in its value proposition. There is a intense rush of innovation to improve the product.
- In Stage 4, the limits of the technology are reached. It is increasingly difficult to squeeze out improvements. For every

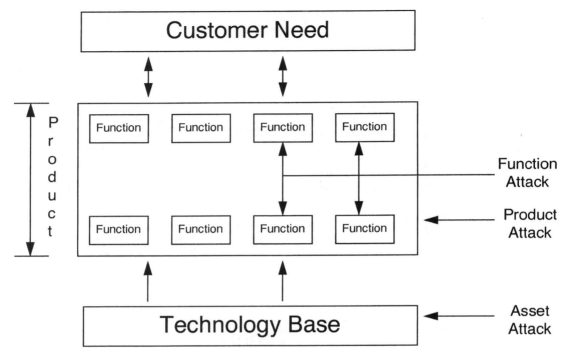

Figure 3.20   **A substitute attack. A substitute attack against an established product may be done at the function level, product level, or asset level.**

dollar invested in R&D, less than a dollar in added value is generated.

Market diffusion also follows an S curve pattern as shown in Figure 3.23. The point at which the diffusion rate is highest is called the point of inflection. At this point, most of the barriers to market acceptance have been overcome and the great horde of imitators follow the aggressive early pioneers. What is particularly interesting is that once the diffusion process starts and achieves a relatively small percentage of market penetration, it almost inevitably goes to completion (unless its attacked by another attacker and becomes a defender). The reason for this is that if the technology provides clear benefits when it is only at the beginning of its S curve, its attraction becomes overwhelming as it dramatically improves as it ascends the S curve.

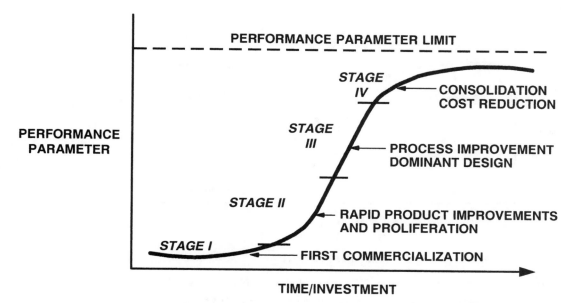

Figure 3.21   S curve. An S curve illustrates the evolution of a product's performance against an specific functional limit. (Source: *The Art of Strategic Planning for Information Technology,* Bernard H. Boar, John Wiley & Sons, Inc., 1993.)

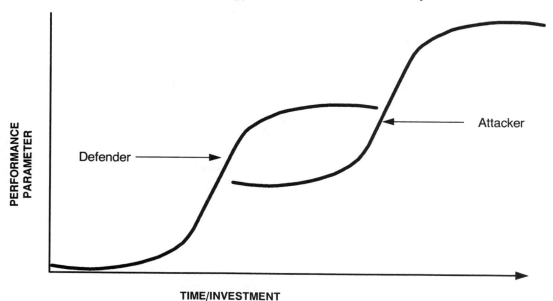

Figure 3.22   Dueling S curves. A substitution situation occurs when a new product on a different S curve challenges an incumbent product.

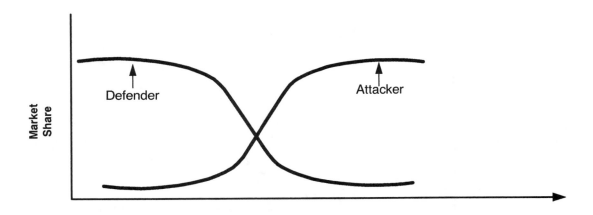

TIME/INVESTMENT

Figure 3.23   **Market diffusion. The market shares of both the attacker and the defender take on an S curve shape as a function of time.**

What normally happens, if there is to be sustained progress for civilization, is that at some point on the S curve, a new technology emerges to challenge it. Fundamental to this replacement technology is that it must have a higher price/performance limit. The attacker, as shown in Figure 3.22, than challenges the defender for the market.

The defender has at least six defenses it can choose in any combination and varying depth:

1. It can search for new and unaffected markets.
2. It can focus on entrenched customers, who will be late, if ever, new product adopters.
3. It can aggressively improve its product (i.e., improve service, lower pricing, improve warranty, etc.).
4. It can raise FUD to stall the migration.
5. It can dramatically increase its R&D in an attempt to generally extend its S curve or focus the R&D for a "function defense." In a function defense, the defender identifies those function clusters that the attacker will have the most difficulty matching, enhances them, and thereby attempts to contain and limit the

substitution to a function attack. This will result in the two products being complementary rather then replacements.

6. It can accept the inevitable and move to the new S curve. This may be done overtly or covertly. When we say covertly, we mean that the product maintains its external name and image but its internals are altered to the attacker's technology. This has certain emotional and psychological advantages with highly committed customers.

In practice, defenders often defend quite poorly, and, if the attacking technology has a superior S curve, its victory is preordained. The reasons for a poor defense are as follows:

- Due to sunken costs, the defender is not willing to abandon her investment.
- The existing technology is politically strong. The organization's power system is not even willing to entertain that an attack is occurring, let alone consider converting.
- The organization's traditions and culture are inwardly focused. It is not conceivable that an alternative solution could exist (i.e., the only real computing is mainframe computing). This results in a very distorted view of the marketplace.
- The organization does not have the will, competencies, or technology assets to change.
- Inertia—the business machine just keeps moving straight ahead, immune to marketplace realities.

In any case, if you study the history of technological substitutions, you will discover that although it may take considerable time to overcome the barriers and climb the S curve, attackers do remarkably well and defenders routinely fail to adopt and become displaced.

Having completed the necessary preparation by this short review of technological substitution and diffusion, we can now proceed to analyze MPS/PSCS assertions in light of our refreshed S curve knowledge. We will do this by presenting an MPS assertion (paraphrased), an exposition of its meaning or implications, and a refutation based on S curve theory.

1. *MPS Assertion:* Mainframes are still whizzing along, performing valuable work, and there is no end in sight.

Implications: The continued existence of mainframes and mainframe applications refutes the notion that mainframes are dead or dying. If C/S was such a powerful replacement, how come my mainframe is still here?

S Curve Refutation: As is obvious from looking at the market diffusion patterns illustrated in Figure 3.23, diffusion is not an event but a multiyear (decades) journey. Some industry analysts suggest that there are over 300 billion lines of mainframe application code.[9] Even if there were no migration question, migration would still be a lengthy and evolutionary process. Given that a typical company spends only 3% of its budget on I/T and 50 to 70% of that budget is for maintenance, how could any type of migration take hold other than over an extended period?

It is typical in technology substitution situations for both the attacker and the defender to coexist for a drawn-out time period. By the MPS argument, mainframes were not replacing EAM equipment because for years EAM equipment still coexisted while the diffusion process occurred. The strategic S curve lesson is not that literal existence ends, it is market share direction. There is no question that the diffusion will take a long time given the large software investment in mainframe technology and its nonportability. The question is not whether you can find examples of mainframes still whizzing along (I can find examples of sailboats whizzing along), the question is on which S curve should you place your next application investment dollar.

As is all too frequently the case, the MPS partisans pick out the right facts but uncannily misinterpret them. Candles are still readily available, horses and buggies can still be found, vacuum tube radios are collector items, steam engine locomotives are still in limited service, structured analysis data flow diagrams and minispecs have not yet turned yellow, and blacksmiths attract very appreciative audiences. The end of the S curve, as the MPS partisans anticipate, is not extinction. The end of the S curve, for the defeated former colossus, is a much harder fate to brave; it is obsolescence. It is very disheartening to live to see your life's work become a museum artifact. It is far superior to remain vibrant rather than to become bitter.[10] So it is best to accept the inevitable, learn the new technology, and jump curves lest you end up an embittered human relic.

2. *MPS Assertion:* C/S can't match my mainframe in functionality. In particular, mainframes are superior for managing large databases and performing large nightly batch runs.

Implications: Since C/S does not provide equal or superior functionality, obviously C/S can't replace my mainframe. Hooray!

S Curve Refutation: IBM is, not surprisingly, executing a function defense. The management of large databases and the execution of large batch jobs are unquestionably two of the strongest functions of mainframe computing. It is not surprising, then, that IBM and its most loyal customers are making a "fortress database/batch" defense. Given that these functions took a long time to develop in the mainframe world, they will probably be the latter functions attacked by C/S.

In essence, the mainframe defense is to move the C/S attack from an asset attack to a function attack. In doing this, IBM is undoubtedly moving its mainframe R&D dollars to further strengthening those functions.[11] In fact, recent IBM announcements such as improved openness with POSIX, DCE, TCP-IP, and DRDA, and putting the mainframe in the business unit called the "Server Group" all indicate this S curve defense. Undoubtedly, it will work for a while. Inevitably, however, there is no reason why batch or large database management can't be done in a fully C/S environment; it is just a question of S curve investments.

An interesting note is that, if one knew in some detail how IBM is spending its mainframe R&D dollars, one would likely see that IBM is not at all confused about what is going on. As is predictable in an S curve challenge, R&D dollars are almost surely going to function defenses (to allow a complementary situation) and covert transition. Whether the MPS likes it or not, within a few years, the coveted mainframe will be converted into C/S technology (CMOS chips). It will have to, because the attack is an asset attack and there really is no long-term defense other than jumping S curves. From a mainframe vendor perspective, however, the longer the duel the better. Why lose one more expensive mainframe MIP to C/S any sooner than they have to?

3. *MPS Assertion:* C/S is not a replacement for mainframes at all. It does nothing better.

Implications: The assertion speaks loudly for itself and requires no amplification.

S Curve Refutation: Let us assume that what the extreme fringe of the MPS is saying is true. Let us assume that C/S is not at all a replacement. This could only mean one of two things: (a) Either all the C/S hardware, software, and communications purchases are not used (they are purchased and immediately put in the basement or thrown into the ocean), or (b) they are used but for different types of applications than are done on mainframes. In either case, C/S is a substitute for neither existing mainframe applications nor the growth of those applications. Mainframe sales should be unaffected.

According to a major market researcher, the cost of mainframe MIPS has dropped from $90,000 in 1990 to $12,000 in 1994. Why such a precipitous drop? A drop that has caused a massive downsizing at IBM and reduced its stock value. Have IBM and its PCM competitors become Santa Claus? The only logical reason for such a precipitous drop and the associated organizational displacements is that substitution is happening. If it wasn't happening, why lower prices? After all, if C/S is no replacement at all, why the need to dramatically cut prices against a noncompetitive product?

The simple truth of course is that a function/asset attack is occurring and making significant progress. IBM defended, as would any defender, by dropping prices. This improves the mainframe's value point and slows the migration by altering the cost/benefit analysis. The S curve scenario is playing out exactly as predicted.

It is interesting to note that, without any gratitude from the MPS beneficiaries, the dramatic unit cost reductions for mainframe computing are the direct consequence of C/S computing. It is the success of CSC in becoming a viable substitute that has caused the decline in mainframe prices. How else can you explain such a significant drop in prices? Under the traditional mainframe competition situation before CSC, IBM and its PCM competitors never would have voluntarily engaged in such self-defeating price reductions. So in an interesting paradox, the MPS is a primary beneficiary of the architecture that they so customarily ridicule.

4. *MPS Assertion:* Functions that have long been solved in the mainframe world are not automated in the C/S environment; therefore, C/S will be very expensive.

Implications: Mainframes have bullet-proof OA&M. Performing OA&M will be very labor intensive in the C/S environment and therefore should dissuade migration.

OA&M Refutation: Bullet-proof production-quality OA&M is unquestionably not as robust today as it is in mainframes. However, there is no inherent reason why it won't be. The communications network is completely distributed and operates quite reliably. While you may not wish to put your most critical applications today on C/S, you have many that could work quite well with imperfectly automated OA&M.

There is no part of the C/S S curve that is more aggressively being attacked than OA&M development. I would suggest that within 2 or 3 years, at most, fully robust OA&M capabilities will exist. If you speak to the C/S vendors, I think you will be pleasantly surprised at the state of OA&M and the plans for improvement. Given the time needed to reengineer an organization for C/S, one is well advised to start the process now so that one can jump at the opportune moment.

An editorial in a major I/T industry newspaper suggested that users not convert to C/S until its OA&M was fully mature and all the C/S vendors had, themselves, moved all their mission critical applications to C/S. This is most interesting advice. What is being suggested is that a new technology not be adopted until it has reached Stage 4 of its S curve; it must be completely risk-free. So you are to remain frozen in a glacial block of mainframe ice until C/S is perfect while your competitors maneuver with less-than-perfect C/S. Did you do this with mainframe computing? Did you wait for it to be perfect or did you struggle to build advantage? As I recall, it took years until the third-party aftermarket vendors created a suite of OA&M tools.

5. *MPS Assertion:* Mainframe MIPS are growing at better than 25% per annum. Not only is the mainframe alive and well, it is experiencing a rebirth and a renaissance.

Implications: This assertion speaks very well for itself and leaves many C/S advocates scratching their heads.

S Curve Refutation: The logic of this assertion would appear initially irrefutable but is sophistry. If the mainframe is growing at over 25%/year, how could it be dying? The answer of course is that a product's market vitality is not a function of inwardly focused sales growth but of market share. That is why market share is such a coveted measure of success. What does it matter if your unit sales grow if the market is growing at twice your rate? Unless your growth exceeds the market rate, as you grow (in unit sales), you decline in market relevance and position (i.e., you are slowly dying).

Figure 3.24 shows typical sales curves for dueling S curve products. Notice that both products may both be growing in unit sales for an extended period. This is quite common in substitution situations for two reasons:

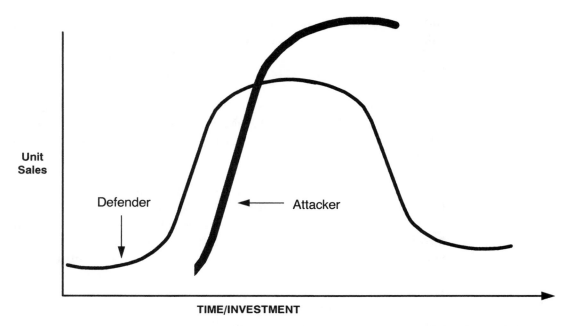

Figure 3.24   Sales curves. It is not unusual for the sales of both the defender and the attacker to be growing at the same time.

1. The new functionality of the challenger, with its complementary relationship to the defender, actually stimulates the defender's demand. Don't you often hear MPS champions saying that CSC is stimulating the demand for mainframes? What they are saying is that the S curve growth of the attacker is arousing sales of the defender because of the complementary functionality. The function defense is, at least temporarily, working, and the defender gets a stay of execution.
2. The diffusion rate is slower than the overall market growth. The rising tide of demand lifts the defender as well as the attacker.

Eventually, however, the attacker continues to grow and the inevitable decline, not only in market share but in unit sales, occurs for the defender.

So you have an interesting paradox: A product may be growing in unit sales but concurrently declining in market share. This is exactly what is happening, and the growth of mainframe MIPS does not at all prove a rebirth or a renaissance. Since the mainframe MIP market share, whether you use total MIPS or server MIPS is in deep decline (free fall), the growth in mainframe MIPS, so cherished and proclaimed by the MPS, actually proves the mainframe's decline, not its resurgence. Contrary to what is normally stated, as mainframe MIPS are growing, mainframes are declining in market share. In fact, as current trends continue, mainframes will become niche technology.

There is not and will not be a rebirth, a renaissance, or a pardon. S curves do not lie; the mainframe's fate is a fait accompli.

SUMMARY

More than anything else, what S analysis can help explain is what is really meant when a mainframe champion asserts that mainframes will never die ("My mainframe will live forever") or when C/S proponents state that mainframes are dead, dying, or dinosaurs. What the mainframe champion means is that mainframes are not subject to S curves. For the first time in the history of technology, there exists a technology that is not subject to limits. Human interfaces and database technology are subject to S curves (Figure 3.25), but not the mainframe. Even more astonishing, it was

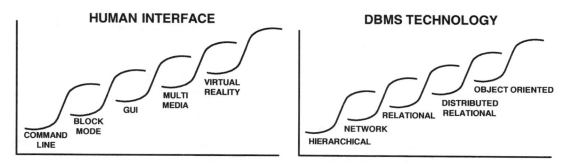

Figure 3.25   Human interface and DBMS S curves. User interfaces and DBMS technologies have been subject to numerous S curve duels. (Source: *The Art of Strategic Planning for Information Technology*, Bernard H. Boar, John Wiley & Sons, Inc., 1993.)

the first S curve of computing, mainframes, that accomplished this feat. If this were true, it would be a most amazing event requiring the most extensive study. Of course, it is nonsense.

When C/S proponents state that mainframes are dead, dying, or dinosaurs, what they mean is crystal clear. What they mean is that a dueling S curve competition is in progress and C/S is winning. Per normal S curve characteristics, winning takes time and is gradual. So when we assert that a mainframe is a dinosaur or dead, we don't mean it should not currently exist, that there will not be continued use in the immediate future, or that mainframe MIPS won't continue to grow. What we mean is that the S curve fate of mainframes is hermetically sealed and you don't have to be a sorcerer or soothsayer to understand what is happening. You just have to understand S curves.

Earlier in this book, I stated that the views of the MPS lacked *strategic acumen*. The absence of S curve thinking and analysis by the mainframe proponents in their assertions, more then any other factor, was the foundation for this statement. S curve theory is a well-established and documented framework for technology evaluation. If the MPS were knowledgeable in S curve theory, how could they even consider making the statements that we refuted? How do they so confidently engage in debate without having performed their strategic homework? Obviously, at least some were not prepared.[12]

Preparation is either required or it is not. If it is not required and you engage in preparation, you waste your time and energy. You waste your time and energy because, having prepared, you are no better off than had you not prepared. Conversely, if preparation is required and you do not prepare, you participate in a sham. You participate in a sham because you engage in debate with a mask of expertise but no substantive expertise. Strategic analysis, in general, and understanding the strategic dimensions of the client/server–mainframe debate in particular, belong to the set of disciplines that demand preparation. The absence of preparation merely clouds the debate with erroneous logic, confuses the listener who is seeking genuine advice and wisdom, and, ultimately, proves embarrassing for the ill-prepared adversary. Sun Tzu said: "Those who face the unprepared with preparation are victorious." Arguments must be formulated not on emotional ties, historical precedents, wishful thinking, or personal tantrums, they must be built on the best preparation possible.

STRATEGIC PARADOX

Why do you need a formal business strategy or an I/T strategy in the first place? Why not, as some would suggest, just wait for a winning strategy to emerge serendipitously or just muddle through? It certainly would be easier than trying to develop a deep and far-reaching vision of the future and then overcoming all the obstacles and barriers to making it happen.

I would suggest that the reason that a prescience strategy is highly alluring is because there are intelligent, proactive, and reactive competitors who seek the identical prize: the customer. Without competition, the conduct of a business reduces to a risk-free administration problem. With competition, the problem of business is not administration but advantage. So the objective of strategy is to win customers but the reason for strategy is competition. This conflict occurs within a climate of extreme conflict of wills and dueling actions and reactions. Without strategy, the conflict takes place as a series of independent tactical encounters without any grand design or plan of how you will ultimately prevail.

Most people in their daily life confront problems by the routine use of *linear thinking* (a.k.a. linear logic). Linear thinking is the utilization of common sense, inductive and deductive reasoning, and the unchallenged desire for optimum efficiency (time, cost, speed, etc.) to select the most direct and efficient way to solve a problem. Few would question this approach. To the contrary, people are ridiculed for not applying common sense, being illogical, or taking a time-consuming circuitous route when a direct path is available. Linear logic is summed up in the idea that if you wish to accomplish A, do the logical sequence of actions that most directly, quickly, and economically leads you to A. Daily and nonconflictual life rewards the efficient, the direct, and the logical.

What experienced strategic thinkers know, however, that most people do not, is that in strategic thinking, linear thinking often leads, paradoxically, to the wrong action. Strategic thinking often demands that the opposite action be taken to what linear thinking would insist upon. Strategic actions take place against a background of intense multidimensional conflict (psychological, economic, spiritual, and physical). Strategists are confronted by an activist opponent who vigorously strives to block, hinder, delay, undo, or reverse their actions. The opponent observes, analyzes, and acts to counter each strategic move. This intense and directed opposition is unusual in routine problem-solving situations. The reversal of logical actions, created as a consequence of the highly adversarial strategic context, is called *strategic paradox.*[13]

Situations of strategic conflict suspend the rules of linear logic and operate within a different set of rules; the rules of strategic paradox. Strategic paradox presents itself in two distinct forms. The first form is called *coming together of opposites.* Coming together of opposites is the phenomenon that, left alone to follow their own natural development, without periodic corrective intervention, strategic actions that start out on a sound linear basis will inevitably migrate to their opposite state. In daily life, this phenomenon is captured in the maxim "You can have too much of a good thing."

Consider the strategic pairs of advantage and disadvantage, alignment and misalignment, and competency and incompetence. Coming together of opposites views each pair as being opposite ends (states) of the same thing. So the ultimate end of advantage is disadvantage, the final end of alignment is misalignment, and the end of competency is incompetence. The mechanics of the strategic paradox of coming together of opposites causes that which originated in sound linear logic to be transmuted into its opposite and undesirable state.[14]

An interesting example of the paradox of coming together of opposites is occuring in the banking industry. Historically, the size of the branch system was a critical advantage for retail banking. Whoever had the greatest consumer reach, by virtue of the number and location of branches, won. With the shift to electronic banking in all its myriad of forms, telephone, PC, interactive television, ATM, internet, etc., the branches are becoming dated and expensive real estate. So that which was the basis of retail banking advantage, the branch system, is becoming the albatross as the foci of retail banking becomes electronic commerce.

So the first idea of strategic paradox, coming together of opposites, is that what causes your success will also cause your failure.[15] Having made you successful, it will, paradoxically, stimulate and motivate your opponents to tax their ingenuity to overcome it. If you become at ease and hold onto it for too long while your opponent develops novel approaches, the reversal occurs, and that which was an advantage becomes a disadvantage. It is dated by the ingenuity of your opponents which was driven by the need to overpower your advantage. So your advantage, ironically, seeds its own ruin.

It is therefore obvious why adept strategists are most worried when a company is at the summit of its success. Inflated with proven advantages, competencies, satisfied customers, and so on, the company grows smug and lazy with that which made it successful. It has reached what may be called the culmination point of its success. Unfortunately, these winning characteristics have the contradictory effect of arousing your opponents to develop entrepreneurial ways to overcome them. If you stand still, self-satisfied and arrogant, the coming together of opposites will take hold and cause you inescapable misfortune.

Excellent strategic thinkers are always vigilant to forestall complacency and self-satisfaction. They know that they must continually infuse exogenous events to disrupt or preempt the coming together of opposites phenomenon from occurring. While many in a winning organization will say to the frantic strategist, "Why tinker with a winning formula?" the strategist will understand that "a winning formula" is but temporary, and is also destined in time to be but "a losing formula." Most will not appreciate the entrapping nature of the strategic paradox of coming together of opposites; while it lures you into a spurious sense of permanent superiority (mainframes will last forever), it concurrently spurs your rivals to new heights of innovation.

Clearly the coming together of opposites has been at work in the demise of mainframe computing. What made it great, a single architecture from a single vendor, now makes it undesirable. It's strength, glass house operation by only an elite group of technologists, is now a weakness. IBM's unparalleled success in completely dominating the market goaded its competitors to develop an alternative architecture built not on proprietary hardware but on software standards and interfaces.

The second form of strategic paradox is called *reversal of opposites*. Reversal of opposites teaches that to accomplish your objectives, you must do exactly the contrary of what sound linear logic suggests. You must suspend common sense and the quest for time or economic efficiency and do the exact opposite. For westerners who pride themselves on rationality, this is certainly a hard concept to accept. It is, nevertheless, correct. The reference maxim of reversal of opposites is contained in the phrase "If you wish peace, prepare for war."[16]

Reversals of opposites logic leads us to the following strategic insights of conflict:

- The best form for an I/T architecture is to be formless.
- Your best competitor should be yourself.
- The best form of confrontation is through indirection and surprise.
- The best barriers to entry attract competitors.

Let us examine the last one in more detail so that you will appreciate the mechanics of reversal of opposites. This idea is certainly paradoxical. Most of us are taught that the best barriers to entry are insurmountable. As routinely taught, a barrier is best when it is impregnable.

Reversal of opposites logic would suggest that by doing this, you force your opponents to be innovative and entrepreneurial. You leave them no choice but to tax their ingenuity to overcome you while, via coming together of opposites, you rest assured on your laurels. Paradoxically, your great barriers seed your own undoing. Competitors do not go away; what they do is regroup and try harder.

Reversal of opposites logic would teach that you should leave some tempting points of entry. Being human and enticed by the simpler approach, your opponent will most likely attack where you have left some room. Yes, you will have to combat your opponent, but it is much better to engage in conflict where you have prepared and chosen the place than for your opponent to out-innovate you. So, paradoxically, by creating imperfect barriers to entry, you entice your opponents to challenge you without exerting their full innovative energy. So the logical thing to do, strong barriers, is really the illogical thing to do, and the illogical thing to do, barriers with tempting holes, is the logical thing to do.

The reason for the reversal of opposites is that conflict reverses the expected rules of daily linear logic. The reversed logic is good logic exactly because it is bad logic. All can prepare for the expected, so strategy in a high-conflict situation demands the unexpected. The thing that must be done is to recognize reversal of opposites situations and act offensively or defensively accordingly.

The paradoxical logic of reversal of opposites is very instructive with regard to understanding and implementing I/T architecture strategically. Conducting business in a free market economy is a high-conflict situation. What it means when one suggests that I/T is to be used strategically is that it is to be a frontline weapon of conflict. The strategic paradox of reversal of opposites will therefore come into play. If you intend to use I/T purely for administrative purposes, then the rules of linear logic will hold. But if you wish to seek strategic advantage from I/T, you must approach your I/T decisions with the logic of paradox.

An I/T architecture, if it is to be the basis of advantage, must anticipate and protect against the inevitable countermeasures of competitors. If competitors can easily replicate, duplicate, or copy what you have done, there is no sustained advantage. Imitation may be the sincerest form of flattery, but it is the most sinister enemy of advantage. So an information architecture that is a solid is of little strategic value at any price. It is too easily understood and countered.

As a strategic weapon, an I/T architecture must be understood and deployed under the logic of strategic paradox. The greater the success of your I/T architecture, the greater the focus, effort and ingenuity of your competitors to leapfrog it. The very success of your architecture generates its own counterforce. To preempt neutralization by your competitors, your architecture must be inscrutable.

Mainframe computing economics has been built on the perfect linear logic of economies of scale. This is done by broad homogeneity and concentration of computing resources. In strategic conflict, however, homogeneity creates vulnerability. It is obvious to all what it is you have done or could do. The perfect linear logic pursuit of economies of scale as the linchpin of strategic computing yields no strategic advantage because all you do is easily decloaked and duplicated.

The commonsense employment of economies of scale thinking as the driver of I/T architecture is not strategic sense at all. Since I/T architecture will sit at the cutting edge of strategic conflict, reversal of opposites teaches that I/T architecture will achieve its maximum strategic value when it is built on rich variety (i.e., computing based on limitless heterogeneity). The paradox of I/T and economies of scale is that economies of scale equates to an efficient but solid I/T when what is required is an incredibly adaptable I/T. Economies of I/T investments are important but must be pursued within the adaptability vector. To use I/T strategically, you must first achieve a broad level of agility. So to concentrate I/T power (big mainframes), you must paradoxically disperse it (CSC); to be efficient (economies of scale), you must first be flexible (economies of sharing). Economic efficiency of strategic I/T only has meaning in the context of a formless I/T.

So strategic paradox teaches us that linear logic holds in nonconflictual circumstances but not in strategic conflicts. This is why mainframe-based I/T has been such a strategic failure. Using linear logic, mainframe computing was optimized for economies of scale but not for variety and inscrutability; there really was no choice given its nature. Mainframe computing could therefore adequately support the nonstrategic administration systems but was a hopeless strategic failure. The strategic failure of mainframe computing, as itemized in Figures 3.6 to 3.12, is therefore not at all surprising. Mainframe computing could not be used strategically because it lacks the attributes of a technology of conflict.

So you must move to client/server because of strategic paradox. Strategic paradox explains the 15-year failure of I/T to make strategic progress. It couldn't make strategic progress because it was proceeding on the wrong logic. Client/server will permit a formless I/T that is appropriate for strategic conflict. Strategic paradox also explains why, in spite of the protest of the MPS and the PSCS, the massive migration to C/S continues. It continues because I/T executives, while they might not formally understand strategic paradox, intuitively do and are acting on that intuition. So I/T executives have not been fooled, mislead, or swindled by self-serving vendors and consultants as the MPS would have us believe. To the contrary, I/T executives have demonstrated brilliant and intuitive strategic astuteness.[17]

I believe, though this is the most difficult argument to accept, that this argument is the most important rationale for moving to CSC. The great advantage of mainframe computing, economies of scale, lauded and revered by the MPS, is really no advantage at all. It is no advantage at all because strategic paradox teaches that incredible variety and agility is the means to strategic advantage at the frontier of conflict.[18] This is why the military does not build just one type of airplane, one type of ship, or one type of tank. Though those solutions would offer the maximum economies of scale, they would also offer the simplest countermeasure to opponents. So the military chooses economics within weapon variety to assure advantage.

The same is true in choosing an I/T architecture. If you intend to use I/T for merely routine administrative tasks, than you should continue to focus on economies of scale and stay with mainframes. If, however, you wish to use I/T strategically, you must put your strategic paradox education into operation and move to a highly amorphous computing architecture. Of course, if your competitors move to client/server and you don't, your intent to use I/T merely for administrative tasks will become irrelevant when they drive you out of business by virtue of maneuver.

An analogy can be helpful in making you feel comfortable with accepting the uncommon sense of strategic paradox and alleviate your skepticism. In Einstein's famous theory of relativity, objects behave as we all expect and have experienced, as long as the objects move at velocities small compared to the velocity of light. However, as an object's velocity approaches the speed of light, weird and bizarre things, in complete contradiction to our normal experiences, happen. For example, as an object approaches the speed of light, from the frame of reference of the viewer to the object,

1. The object shrinks in length.
2. The mass of the object increases.
3. Time dilates and slows down.

The values of these variables, to our disbelief and astonishment, are not constant but a function of frame of reference and speed. While this clashes without common sense and is difficult to believe, this is the scientific accepted explanation of motion at speed of light like velocities.

So what Einsteins's theory teaches us is that the behavior of objects is a function of speed. Our commonsense perceptions of motion are based on a slow moving experience. If we lived in a world where objects routinely approached the speed of light, these weird and bizarre behaviors would not be weird and bizarre at all but be mundane experiences taken for granted and not given a second thought.

The same would seem to be true with regard to linear logic. What is logical and illogical is not a constant but a function, not of speed, but of intensity of conflict. Since in or daily lives we primarily experience little conflict, the commonsense rules of linear logic hold and we act accordingly. In intense conflictual situations, however, the rules of logic change; they become weird and bizarre. What is a logical behavior is a function of intensity of conflict. So logical actions are to conflict as behaviors of objects in motion are to speed. Though our common sense fails us, it fails us only because our normal experiences are in a limited segment of the possible set of experiences. Objects moving near to speed of light do not act bizarre, they act as they should at that speed. Similarly, strategic paradox is not paradox at all. In intense conflict, the non-conflict commonsense illogical is the high conflict logical. So the strategic reversal of opposites paradox, "To concentrate computing power, you must disperse it, " is not a paradox at all. It is the correct linear logic for the domain of high intensity conflict.

So to understand and formulate I/T strategy, you must understand strategic paradox, but to understand strategic paradox, you must understand Einstein's theory of relativity. It therefore follows logically that to formulate I/T strategy, you must understand the theory of relativity. Now that is really weird and a conclusion that I am sure that neither you nor I ever expected to reach.

The conclusions of this argument are straightforward, even if not easily accepted. Whether you are pursuing a differentiation strategy or a cost-advantage strategy for the business, I/T, as a strategic weapon, is subject not to linear logic but the laws of strategic paradox. The reason that I/T has been and will continue indefinitely to be a discouraging strategic fiasco is that linear logic leads, paradoxically, to the optimization of the wrong variables. What is required is heterogeneity, not homogeneity. What is needed is flexibility and then economies, not economies then flexibility. Mainframe computing has always had it strategically backwards. I suggest you carefully mull this over for a while.

VISION

Most business leaders recognize the critical importance of a winning business vision to success. A vision is a clear and compelling image of the future that attracts employee respect, enthusiasm, and excitement. It defines winning. It is normally quite different from a transparent and simple linear extrapolation of the present and requires major changes in how a business operates. A compelling vision garners the most important of all elements for success: commitment, belief, and effort.

What is the MPS vision for I/T? After you complete reading the MPS literature and listening to their spokespeople at leading seminars, what is the clear and compelling vision of the future that they offer us to excite our employees to stretch and struggle for advantage? I believe the final sentence in *The Dinosaur Myth*[19] provides an excellent summary of the MPS vision:

> Those who dismiss mainframes as dinosaurs should remember
> that mainframes have existed in their present form for 40 years at
> most and dinosaurs ruled the earth for 160 million years.

It would seem that the vision that we are offered is 159,960,000
more years of computing, more or less, in its present form. Is this a
vision of innovation and entrepreneurship or a vision for people
who have decided to coast on yesterday's glories? Is this a vision
that understands S curves or value propositions? Is this a vision
that will enable us to maneuver? This is a vision of simple extrapolation of what has happened without any imagination of what
could be done to make us great. It offers no prescience of a winning
future. It is shallow and nearsighted.

What is the vision of CSC? Strategically understood, CSC offers
the following imposing vision:

- Flexible, responsive, adaptive, and fast I/T.
- Perfect reach, range, and maneuverability to enable the business to negotiate the business environmental diversity.
- Systematic I/T where it is needed, when it is needed, how it is
  needed, and in the exact amounts needed.

The CSC vision is compelling, exciting, and worth the extended
commitment of your staff. A vision of formless I/T that perfectly
adapts to the dynamics of the business rather than the business
adapting to a rigid I/T. A vision of I/T as a changeling, not a solid;
a vision that is deep and far-reaching.

Sun Tzu said

> Vision is seeing victory before it exists.
> This is the strategist way to strategic triumph.

The MPS offers us more of what everyone knows. This is not, has
never been, and will never be the path to victory. Close your eyes
and think of 159 million more years of host-based computing. Can
you stand before your peers and recount to them the story of your
future victories? When I close my eyes and imagine a world of
CSC, I see all kinds of opportunities for advantage that have not
yet taken shape. Seeing the formless before it is visible to all is what
is required of visionary management. So close your eyes and imagine competing, not with monolithic computing but with a strategic

configuration of power that permits you to be extraordinarily flexible and adaptable. Close your eyes and see strategic triumph.

Always remember, "Vision is seeing victory before it exists." If you follow the advice of the MPS, you will see victory when it is too late; after your opponents have long since mastered and implemented CSC. You will be technologically safe, having jumped to CSC at the top of the S curve, but you will sorry. You will be sorry because your company will be in a hopeless death spiral—outmaneuvered and unable to compete with those who can cope with the value chain in a vastly superior manner.

SUMMARY

Having presented these arguments around the world, I would not be at all surprised if your initial reaction is one of surprise. Most of the standard arguments in favor of CSC are fairly simple and straightforward (i.e., adopt C/S because of declining unit costs of microprocessors or because CSC is flexible).

It is my belief that CSC is not just another computing technology but a watershed event. It therefore demands a deep and far-reaching analysis so that a deep and far-reaching implementation plan may be formulated. If the analysis is inadequate, the strategy will not be right and no amount of heroic effort will compensate in implementation for a broken strategy.

The MPS and the PSCS are guilty of muddle-headed thinking. As you now understand from the material presented, many of their arguments don't even qualify as good nonsense. S curve analysis, in particular, demonstrates the lack of depth and preparation of their arguments.

The core rebuttal to the MPS/PSCS assertions are as follows:

- Mainframe computing has been a strategic failure. As a consequence, its value proposition is extremely poor. There is every reason to believe that the migration to CSC would continue, albeit more slowly, even if mainframe computing was free. CSC offers a premium value proposition.
- Confronted with global competition, business is moving from national wars of attrition to global wars of maneuver. The I/T assets must align with the new business style. Even if mainframe computing was appropriate for an attrition market

style, it has no record of being able to support a maneuver style. C/S is, to the contrary, an ideal architecture to support global wars of maneuver.

- S curve analysis provides numerous insights into the inner nature of the mainframe–C/S controversy. What is going on is not some unusual event but the normal process of technological substitution and diffusion. We are well along the substitution/diffusion cycle, and the death of monolithic host-based computing is clearly foretold. It is not foretold because the PC lunatic fringe wishes it to be so or the UNIX crazies are in revolt, but because the mechanics and dynamics of technological substitution and diffusion say so.

- Strategic paradox provides the basis for the logic of conflict. If I/T is to be deployed as a strategic weapon, it is subject to the laws of coming together of opposites and reversal of opposites. We therefore assert, in full recognition of the linear logic paradox, that the heterogeneous and the flexible are required instead of the solid and the efficient. Regardless of your social, political, or emotional ties to mainframe computing, the rules of strategic paradox cannot be abrogated or nullified by your wishful thinking to persevere with mainframe computing forever.

- Vision provides the platform for future victories. CSC offers a deep and far-reaching vision for the future. Mainframe computing offers more of the boring and unsuccessful same.

All these assertions are fully compatible with our previous statement that the overarching challenge to I/T is to overlay incredible flexibility on environmental business diversity (Figure 2.17). This is done through a reach, range, and maneuverable architecture that has CSC at its core (Figure 3.18).

EPILOGUE

In the summer of 1994, while participating in a Bell Laboratories seminar in Holmdel, New Jersey, for our Northeastern customers, an executive raised her hand and said that all of this was well and good but that her senior management didn't wish to change one iota. They were quite content with how things were, and she couldn't imagine a scenario that could make them budge an inch.

Without forethought, I leaned as far forward on the podium as I dare and said, quite spontaneously, *"But, they will come!"* There was a sudden hush in the audience as the implications of what I said sunk in. Sun Tzu said

> What causes opponents to come of their own accord is the prospect of gain. What discourages opponents from coming is the prospect of harm. So the rule is not to count on opponents not coming, but to rely on having ways of dealing with them; not to count on opponents not attacking, but to rely on having what cannot be attacked.

The greater your success, the greater the assurance that they will come (strategic paradox). They might not come today or tomorrow but they will come. They always have and they always will.

The issue of migrating to C/S is therefore an eminently practical question. It is a question of survival. When they come, and you may be sure that they will, will you be prepared to parry their advance? When they attack maneuver style, attacking anywhere and everywhere, what will be the strategic configuration of your response?

NOTES

1. For a detailed analysis of how CSC provides therapy for the chronic strategic I/T problems see *Implementing Client/Server Computing: A Strategic Perspective*, Bernard H. Boar, McGraw-Hill, 1993.
2. An attrition fighter attempts to mass her superior physical assets against the assets of her opponent for a decisive victory. A maneuver fighter attempts to mass her assets against fragments of her opponents assets. In this way, although you are smaller overall, at the point of the confrontation, you are bigger.
3. For a thorough discussion of a reach, range, and maneuverability architecture see *Practical Steps for Aligning Information Technology with Business Strategies*, Bernard H. Boar, John Wiley & Sons, 1994. The original notions of reach and range were introduced by P. Keen in *Shaping the Future*, Harvard Business School Press, 1991.
4. Sun Tzu said

> A victorious strategy is not repeated, the configurations of response to the enemy are inexhaustible. . . .Water configures its flow in accord with the terrain; the army controls its victory in accord with the enemy. Thus, the army does not maintain any

constant strategic configuration of power; water has no constant shape. The end of an army's form is formlessness.

If I/T is to be deployed strategically, it must become formless. When it becomes formless, against what do your opponents attack and against what do they defend? So the correct metaphor for an I/T architecture is water (CSC), not ice (mainframe computing). When you overlay reach, range, and maneuverability on your business environmental diversity, your I/T architecture becomes the means of inexhaustible responses and initiatives. You should worry less about what your I/T architecture costs and more about its ability to serve as your strategic configuration of I/T power.

5. The process through which an individual product undergoes successive refinement is called "successive or advancing generations." In I/T jargon, we refer to this routine occurrence as "releases."

6. See Appendix E for a technological substitution and diffusion bibliography.

7. Multiple substitution events could be occurring simultaneously. For our purposes, we will limit our discussion to the situation of a single defender and a single attacker at a time.

8. S curves are also referred to as sigmoid curves, pearl curves, logistic curves, and Gompertz curves. The first publication with S curves dates back to 1925. See Appendix E for an S curve bibliography.

9. This would include not only procedural languages (COBOL, Assembler, PL/1, FORTRAN) but job control language statements, utility statements, screen definition statements, sort/merge statements, report writer definitions, fourth generation languages, database definition languages, and so on.

10. An interesting example of this is portrayed at the end of the play *Amadeus*. Salieri, who was the most celebrated composer in Europe during his prime, lives to see his music become obsolete and replaced by his archrival Mozart. I would imagine the proponents of the structured techniques of the 1970s are having a similar sad experience.

11. At an industry conference that held a debate between a mainframe advocate and a C/S partisan, the C/S partisan argued that mainframe computing was "intellectually dead." This was dismissed as being meaningless but is actually quite insightful. Mainframe computing is intellectually dead because there is a minimum amount of R&D being invested in mainframe computing. R&D dollars are being diverted to either a function defense or C/S conversion.

12. A number of years ago, there was an intermittent debate between proponents of MVS JCL and the UNIX Shell language as to which is superior. Imagine a fictitious debate in which the Shell partisan stated the following:

- JCL has no condition code checking capability.
- JCL has no referback capability.
- JCL has no variable substitution capability.
- JCL may only allocate disk space in units of cylinders.
- JCL has no way to specify a nullfile situation.

Obviously, the MVS participant would conclude that the problem is not an honest difference of opinions but a complete lack of preparation and knowledge by her adversary. She may infer that her adversary, in JCL parlance, is a "DD dummy" and has been glib in her arguments.

Since S curve analysis is both so relevant to the issue at hand and a well-established and proven analytical method, its complete absence from the MPS arguments implies a similar glibness. Its glaring absence signals a lack of considered preparation by the MPS partisans.

13. For the best explanation of strategic paradox, see E. Luttwak, *Strategy*, Belknap Press, 1987.

14. Sun Tzu said, "Disorder arises from order, cowardice arises from courage, weakness arises from strength."

15. For an excellent article that explains how the greater the business success, the greater the ultimate business failure, see D. Miller, "The Architecture of Simplicity," *Academy of Management Review*, Vol. 18, No. 1, 1993.

16. The converse would also seem paradoxically true; if you wish to defeat your opponent with the absolute minimum expenditure of effort, attack them with an all-encompassing and extended peace. An expansive peace will atrophy their ability and will to fight. Once it has reached its nadir, your opponent can be overcome with the least effort and force. So the rule of optimum efficiency in the world of strategic paradox is *to achieve the absolute most, do the absolute least*.

17. I guess we won't have to wear scarlet letters after all.

18. Since S curves live at the boundaries of conflict, it is not surprising that they exhibit a number of paradoxes:

- As a product accelerates through the high growth portion of the S curve and achieves ever-greater market share, it, paradoxically, also approaches its limits.
- Once a successful S curve attack has begun, a defender can be growing in unit sales but be declining in market share. So while they are growing in units sold, they are dying in market share.
- As the attacker succeeds, it paradoxically both causes the defender to lower its prices to the benefit of those who will not convert and stimulates sales of the defender because of complementary functionality. The laggards, paradoxically, disparage the attacking technology but benefit from it in terms of the improved value propositions it forces from the defender.
- Before sales plumet, the defender, paradoxically, enjoys a final huge sales surge. The "super nova" effect is caused by the emotional ties of customer decision makers to the dying technology.

The more a technology sits at the edge of conflict, the more it must be understood and managed in terms of paradox.

19. *The Dinosaur Myth*, Xephon, 2nd edition.

4

The Economics of Client/Server Computing

Without fear of rebuttal or contradiction, the most defamatory accusation that has been leveled at CSC is the charge that CSC is significantly more expensive than host-centered computing and that this premium relationship will remain so indefinitely. No accusation in the field of computing is as odious and injurious to one's reputation as being labeled *costly*. With the publication in the last few years of a set of independent studies that assert, at worst, a 14.3 to 1 cost disadvantage for CSC, the spendthrift nature of CSC is now an established "fact" (though in truth it is a fiction).

To review from Chapter 1 (see Appendixes A and B), the cost assertions of the MPS are as follows:

- Client/server computing is significantly more expensive than mainframe computing and will continue to be so indefinitely.
- CSC is, at best, equal to host-based computing, at worst is 14.3 times as expensive, and is most likely 3 to 4 times as expensive.
- The cost premium is due to "hidden costs," the lack of OA&M tools, and the overall labor intensity of CSC.
- Mainframe computing is inherently cheaper by virtue of being driven by economies of scale that are not available to CSC. CSC by virtue of its structure cannot be cheaper and must be more expensive.
- Improvements in C/S economics are slowing relative to mainframe computing, and continued improvements in host-centered computing will widen the cost gap.

This attack has been quite successful: The mainframe community has rejoiced (they have been vindicated and were right all along), and C/S advocates have run for cover and sought shelter in justifying C/S by soft noneconomic benefits.

This libel must not be ignored. Less cost (i.e., cost savings, cost reduction, cost avoidance, and cost efficiency) is the pervasive theme of our era. For most decision makers, when push comes to shove, cost is the driving force of decision making. We can therefore not permit this defamation to go unchallenged. All the other criticisms of C/S are miserably weak seconds to this issue. The FUD (fear, uncertainty, and doubt) raised about the economics of C/S must be lifted, the record set straight, and the good name of C/S restored.

Before we begin the arguments for the defense, it should be noted that there are many studies and affidavits by C/S converts that do document significant cost savings. These studies and experiences are challenged by the MPS on the following grounds:

- They are self-serving. The people who decided to implement C/S are the same people who declare the laudatory results. It is therefore not surprising that they declare successes.
- The cost analyses are methodologically flawed. Key cost elements are missing, and questionable assumptions skew the results.
- The studies ignore, to their benefit, "hidden costs." If they accounted for all the labor costs of the end users, the results would be quite different.
- The studies compare apples to oranges. Consequently, they prove nothing.

Of course, the MPS cost studies do not suffer from these or any other methodological flaws, but we will address that issue later.

SOURCES OF ECONOMIC EFFICIENCY

The fundamental flaw in the mathematics of the studies that assert that CSC is more dear than host-centered computing is that they apply a cost analysis model that, while appropriate for host-centered computing, is inappropriate for CSC. There are four primary sources of economic savings and efficiencies:

1. *Economies of Scale:* The decline of average costs per unit of product due to increases in production volume per unit of time.

2. *Economies of Scope:* The reduction of average costs per unit of product by the addition of another product to the product portfolio.
3. *Economies of Learning/Experience:* The decline in average costs per unit of production due to improved quality, excellence, or design of the product by virtue of learning and experience.
4. *Economies of Sharing:* The decline in average cost per unit due to increased efficiencies of reuse. Efficiencies are achieved by reducing the consumed units of production rather than the cost per unit.

Host-centered computing has, unquestionably and correctly, built its cost structure on economies of scale. The cost structure of CSC is constructed on economies of sharing. No cost model is inherently better to apply than another. It is the inappropriate application of economies of scale to C/S costing that has led to the erroneous studies. When economies of sharing is used as the basis for costing C/S, the results are very favorable to C/S. Fair and valid cost comparisons must be made using the appropriate cost model for each contestant.

THE ECONOMICS OF SHARING

The production of information is the goal of I/T.[1] Businesses and other institutions are massively parallel information processing factories (see Figure 2.14) whose primary or adjunct function is the collection, transport, storage, processing, and dissemination of information in all its varied forms. Information can therefore be understood as a manufacturing commodity, and commodity cost analysis can be used to determine the most cost-efficient architecture to manufacture information.

The cost of information (C_i) is the sum of the cost of using information (C_u) and the cost of maintaining information (C_m). C_u consists of the costs of locating, retrieving, and processing information. C_m consists of the costs of creating and maintaining the information. So $C_i = C_u + C_m$.

Figure 4.1 illustrates the general cost function curves for manufactured commodities as a function of architecture. The following variables are defined:

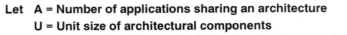

Let **A = Number of applications sharing an architecture**
U = Unit size of architectural components
S = Probability that architectural components can be shared

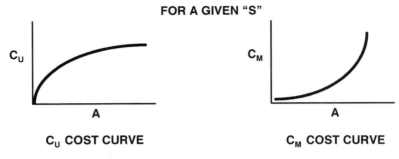

FOR A GIVEN "S"

C_U C_M

A   A

C_U COST CURVE   **C_M COST CURVE**

GENERAL SHAPE OF COST   **GENERAL SHAPE OF COST**
FOR USING INFORMATION   **FOR MAINTAINING INFORMATION**

Figure 4.1   Individual commodity cost function curves. The general commodity cost curves for C_u and C_m are inverse to each other. [Source: *Information Cost as a Determinant of System Architecture*, Levent Orman, Information and Software Technology, 36 (3), 1994.]

- *A*, the number of applications that can share an architecture.
- *U*, the unit size of architectural components. It is our assumption that the size of *U* and the relationships of *U* components to each other, their topology, is a primary driver of architecture cost.
- *S*, the probability that architectural components, *U*, can be shared.

Notice that the cost curves for C_u and C_m are inverse to each other. Figure 4.2 illustrates the derived C_i cost curve by adding C_u and C_m together from Figure 4.1.

Figure 4.3 illustrates the effect of varying *U* on both C_u and C_m. For C_u, due to economies of access, large *U* is cheapest. For C_m, due to economies of sharing, small *U* is cheapest. Figure 4.4 illustrates the derived C_i cost curve for variable *U* by adding the cost curves in Figure 4.3 together. Notice in Figure 4.4 that for a low value of *A*, large *U* is cheapest, while as *A* increases, there is a transition point and then small *U* is cheapest.

Let A = Number of applications sharing an architecture
U = Unit size of architectural components
S = Probability that architectural components can be shared

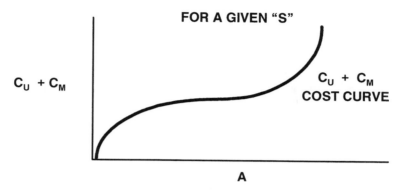

**GENERAL SHAPE OF COST FOR USING
AND MAINTAINING INFORMATION**

Figure 4.2 C_i cost curve. This curve is derived by adding the C_u and C_m curves from Figure 4.1 together. [Source: *Information Cost as a Determinant of System Architecture,* Levent Orman, Information and Software Technology, 36 (3), 1994.]

Figure 4.5 divides the cost curve into the area where host-centered computing has the cost advantage and the area where C/S has the cost advantage. If you have a small number of applications, small A, sharing the architecture, then C_u dominates the cost equation and host-centered computing is cheaper. However, as A increases (i.e., your sharing increases), C_m dominates the cost equation and C/S is cheaper. But why are you moving to C/S in the first place? Is it to build another generation of standalone applications or is it to enable enterprise-wide sharing of information and processing services both within the enterprise and with its value chain partners? Is it not by the decoupling of high-value services and positioning them as reusable servers that flexibility and maneuverability are achieved?

All the cost analyses that have been offered which show C/S to be more expensive are founded on the cost of moving "an" appli-

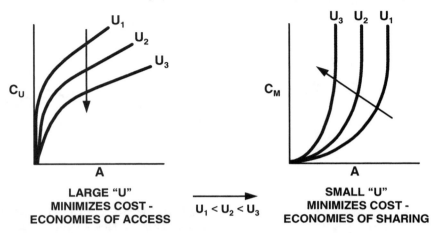

Figure 4.3 Cost curves for variable U. For C_u, large U is cheapest but for C_m, small U is cheapest. [Source: *Information Cost as a Determinant of System Architecture*, **Levent Orman, Information and Software Technology, 36 (3), 1994.**]

cation or group of applications, as is, without rearchitecting, to C/S. They assume that you will not rearchitect to take advantage of economies of sharing and will repeat the architectural isolation of the host-centered world. C/S will be cheaper because as you share and reuse, which is what you want to do, C/S savings will kick in as a critical mass of applications are added to the shared architecture. In fact, if you look at Figure 4.5, you will see that you will be able to deliver information that is not deliverable at any cost with host-centered computing.

Ironically, the MPS cost analyses are in complete agreement with this analysis. All of the MPS analyses exemplified small A migrations to C/S, and, as the cost curve predicts, C/S was more expensive. The thinking, however, was mainframe constrained. They did not go further in their thinking because they maintained economies of scale as the sole basis for costing. As shown in Figure 4.5, as the kindling mass of sharing occurs, tremendous cost savings will occur. So the hallowed cost studies that prove that client/server is

Let **A = Number of applications sharing an architecture**
U = Unit size of architectural components
S = Probability that architectural components can be shared

For a given "S"

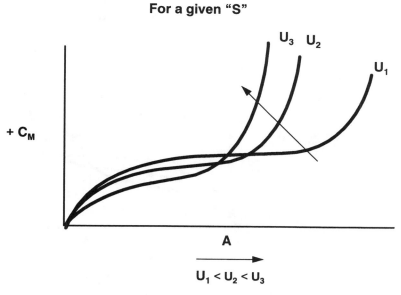

Figure 4.4 C_i cost curve as a function of variable U. This curve is derived by adding the C_u and C_m curves from Figure 4.3 together. [Source: *Information Cost as a Determinant of System Architecture*, Levent Orman, Information and Software Technology, 36 (3), 1994.]

more expensive than host-centered computing prove no such thing at all. What they prove is that if you do not understand the economics of C/S and move to C/S without rearchitecting for massive sharing, you will incur additional cost. However, since the underlying motivation for moving to C/S is flexibility and sharing, why wouldn't you architect to be aligned with the new computing model? Why manage the C/S environment with host-centered thinking? When you jump S curves, it is common to have to rethink your whole approach to using the new technology. Costing is just another part of that global rethinking.

At this point, many objections are raised. What about the labor intensity? What about the hidden costs? What about the lack of

Let   A = Number of applications sharing an architecture
      U = Unit size of architectural components
      S = Probability that architectural components can be shared

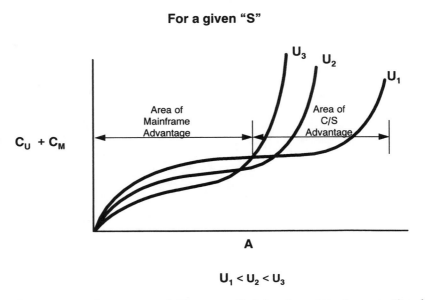

For a given "S"

$U_1 < U_2 < U_3$

Figure 4.5 C_i segmented. For a small A, host-centered computing has
the cost advantage, but as A increases, C/S has the cost
advantage.

sophisticated OA&M? As you will recall from the previous chapter,
C/S is on the high-slope part of the S curve. This part is driven by
the Entrepreneurial Cycle, as shown in Figure 4.6. A tremendous
amount of innovation and entrepreneurism is being applied to
addressing these issues. As they are individually and collectively
addressed, the cost curve will be moving swiftly to the left.

Our MPS colleagues forget that it was this entrepreneurial cycle
that fixed the similar shortcomings in the host-centered environment. Figure 4.7 shows a partial list of OA&M tools that were deriv-
atives of the mainframe S curve. The same thing is happening with
C/S. In fact, in another interesting paradox, the very labor intensity
that the MPS complains about guarantees that it will be eliminated
in short order. It is the smell of profits that attracts entrepreneurs
and innovators, and they are rushing to meet the challenge. Within

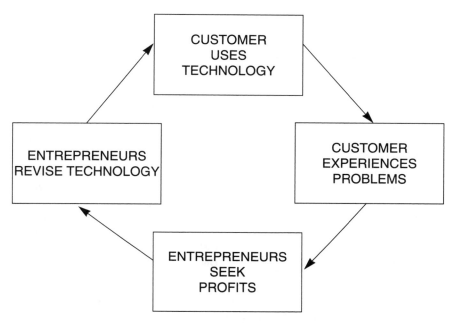

Figure 4.6   **The entrepreneurial cycle. The entrepreneurial cycle is addressing the shortcomings of C/S and rapidly propelling the savings point to the left.**

two years at the most, there will be quite elaborate tools to address these issues and dramatically shift the savings point to the left. While some MPS spokespeople suggest that it will take an extraordinary amount of time and will be extremely difficult to have production grade OA&M for C/S, why should this be the case? The communications network is completely distributed, yet its reliability, availability, and maintainability are taken for granted.

Your strategy, therefore, is to move to C/S, with its *labor intensity,* and ride the S curve (i.e., do exactly what you did with mainframe computing). With mainframe computing, did you wait until it was perfect to pursue advantage or did you build advantage and then address shortcomings with the after-market products and services that emerged? If you wait until C/S is at the top of its S and it is perfectly safe, you will have waited much too long, as all your competitors will be able to radically outmaneuver you. Advantage is not built on safety, it is built on vision, risk, boldness, effort, pru-

Product	Vendor	Function
Omegamon II–IMS	Candle	OA&M and TP monitor
Omegamon – MVS	Candle	OA&M
IMF (6 products)	Boole & Babbage	All functions
IMS DB Tools (4 products)	IBM	DBMS Support
IMSPARS	IBM	Performance
DataPacker	BMC	DBMS / Performance
Image Copy +	BMC	DBMS
Loadplus	BMC	DBMS
Unload +	BMC	DBMS
Recovery +	BMC	DBMS
Prefix Res +	BMC	DBMS
IMS Fast Path Utilities	BMC	DBMS / Performance
Delta IMS	BMC	TP Monitor

Figure 4.7   **Entrepreneurial amnesia. Our MPS colleagues forget how the drivers of S curve improvements, innovation, and entrepreneurism provided solutions for labor intensity in the host-centered world.**

dence, reason, and imagination. There is no safety for the business in the turbulent marketplaces in which it must compete, and there is no safety either for strategic I/T.

There are some instructive analogies with regard to achieving savings through economies of sharing rather than economies of scale. Back in the primordial period of I/T, each application had its own private file system (Figure 4.8a). The database prophets came forth and told us that to improve the quality of the data and to incur savings, we must move to database technology. Many followed the database prophets but, unfortunately, merely replaced private file systems with private databases (Figure 4.8b). This resulted in an increase in data management costs and all kinds of studies proving conclusively that database technology was more expensive than file systems. At the next year's seminar, the besieged prophets told us that it was not enough to replace file systems by databases, the new databases must be shared (Figure 4.8c). They were, of course, right: By sharing datastores, all kinds of I/T expenses due to redundancy were eliminated. So it was not enough to just move to database technology and literally replace file sys-

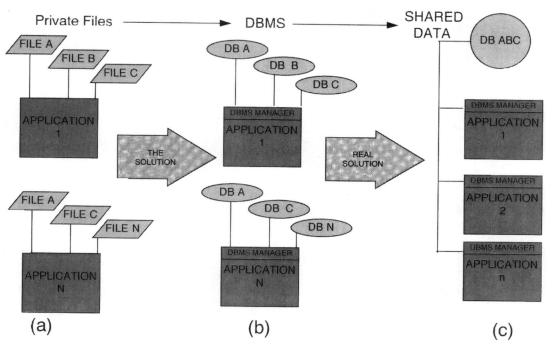

Figure 4.8   Database management. Database technology didn't offer savings over file systems until database sharing was introduced.

tems with databases, it was necessary to rearchitect how you fundamentally managed data. You had to move from nonsharing to sharing to realize the benefits and savings.

The same sequence of learning would seem to be occurring with object oriented programming. Most programs today are either spaghetti code or structured code (Figure 4.9a). The object oriented prophets have told us that we can accrue gigantic savings by moving to object oriented programming. Unfortunately again, as shown in Figure 4.9b, most early attempts at object oriented programming have been at a singular application level. The results, as would be expected, have been bellows that object oriented programming is more expensive due to the increased design effort and overhead in passing data between objects. Are the spaghetti programmers vindicated and is object oriented programming a waste of time and effort? Of course not. The solution (Figure 4.9c) is that objects must be shared across numerous applications. It is through

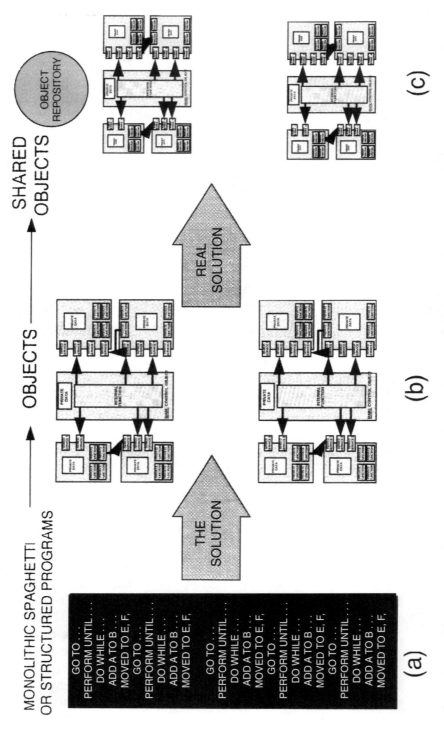

Figure 4.9   Object oriented programming. Object oriented programming will provide savings over conventional programming techniques only when program objects are extensively shared.

sharing that objects deliver savings. So again, it is not enough to literally replace structured programming with object oriented programming: You must rearchitect your programming methods to encourage and reward sharing through shared object repositories.

It would therefore seem that a new paradigm for economic computing is emerging. Rather than trying to save money through brute force economies of scale, as we go forward, the leading companies will minimize I/T expenses through concatenated layers of sharing (i.e., architecture sharing through C/S technology, data sharing through shared database servers, and logic sharing through object oriented programming repositories). They will minimize expenses through leverage.[2]

An important side point of this analysis is to always remember that technology is inert and inanimate. The success of technology is as much, if not more, associated with the implementation strategy as it is with the inherent feature/functionality of the technology. In the great strategy classic, *The Five Rings* by Musashi Miyamoto, he argues the simple but profound truth that a great warrior with a poor sword will be invincible while a mediocre warrior with a great sword will be easily defeated. Victory lies fundamentally within the warrior, not with his weaponry.

The same would seem to be true with information technology. While it is convenient and expedient to blame technology for implementation failures, it is as often the truth that the failing lies with the implementers. I recall a number of years ago when relational databases were engaged in their "S" curve attack on hierarchical databases that an article appeared in an I/T magazine lamenting the failure of a relational databases project. Upon reading the article, I discovered that the implementation team did not do physical design reviews, did not do a prototype, did not do volume testing, and did not hire any assistance even though it was their first relational project. The problem here was certainly not relational technology but the amateurish skills of the project team.

Imagine creating a spreadsheet in which you inadvertently substitute additions for subtractions and the converse. After running the spreadsheet and observing the obvious erroneous results, you check the spreadsheet and discover the coding error. Is the problem the spreadsheet or your algorithm? If your expectations have not been met with your client/server projects in terms of cost savings, flexibility or other (portability, scalability, vendor independence, etc.), is the problem your client/server or your implementation algorithm?

As more and more emerging technologies have to be implemented and integrated into the technology portfolio, all and any approaches will not suffice. It really does matter how you understand the technology and how you design its implementation. Databases, client/server, object oriented, and all the others that will be forthcoming will only be as good as the insight and wisdom used in their deployment.

SOME ASIDES

A few additional items must be reviewed to round out our costing argument:

1. I/T savings from migrating to C/S is primarily driven by I/T architecture and sharing. If you simply move an application, as is, to a downsized platform, your prospects for savings are iffy. If you mindlessly put a GUI front on an existing application, your prospects for savings are iffy. If you redesign a mainframe application in isolation and move it to client/server, your prospects for savings are iffy. However, if you first redesign your I/T architecture to promote sharing and than move a family of applications to that architecture, your prospects for savings are excellent. So of all the "re"s, (*re*novate, *re*write, *re*locate, *re*place, *re*design, and *re*architect), only rearchitecting at the application family level assures huge savings.

2. The savings are undoubtedly supported by the underlying economic advantages of C/S technology (i.e., cheaper MIPS, cheaper storage, etc.). These raw savings (see Figures 1.2 to 1.4) explain why, in some cases, nonsharing migrations still result in savings. In these cases, the brute cost savings of C/S technology overshadow any additional expenses for OA&M, labor, or "hidden costs."

3. It should be recognized that given a choice of economic approaches (i.e., economies of scale or economies of sharing) in the case of I/T, economies of sharing is a highly preferable approach. Economies of scale, unintentionally, often reward "bad" behaviors. Consider a new application that is being built where the measure of success is economies of scale. The developers choose not to reuse existing databases or services and redundantly re-create everything. When the application is

implemented, there is a massive increase in resources and unit costs decline through even greater economies of scale. The operations management announces how they have again reduced the cost of computing. Consider the standard benchmark that is done for mainframe data centers. The benchmarking company maintains a database of unit costs as a function of total MIPS, total storage, total lines of print, and so on. The resources of the client are evaluated, and the unit costs of the client are measured against the reference companies based on size. The more interesting question is never asked: Should we be using so many MIPS, so much storage, and so forth in the first place? So while mainframe computing, driven by economies of scale rewards ever-greater scale, client/sever computing, driven by economies of sharing, rewards ever-greater sharing. The whole psychology of development and operations is not to build more but to reuse. Host-centered computing, again, has it backward. The best way to reduce costs is not to use ever-more resources, even at declining unit costs, but not to use additional resources in the first place. We might say that C/S achieves cost savings by the art of not doing. So if total cost equals number of units times cost/unit, C/S emphasizes dramatically reducing the number of units while mainframe computing rewards reducing the cost/unit through increasing the number of consumed units.

4. The typical MPS cost analysis assigns the cost of architecture infrastructure to each project. This front loads the costs of these projects and would seem to be inconsistent with the teachings of economics with regard to "externalities." Externality theory is concerned with the impacts of transactions on third parties. A negative externality occurs when two parties engage in a transaction and it has a negative impact on a noninvolved third party. A positive externality occurs when two parties engage in a transaction and it has a positive effect on a non-involved third party.

When developers choose an architecture for their application, if they choose other then the approved standard architecture, they engage in a negative externality. After all, they are happy and the selected vendors are happy. The only ones unhappy are the third party corporate architecture people. They are therefore pressured to choose the corporate architecture. When they choose the corporate architecture, they engage in a positive externality; they perform a public good for which they really do not receive direct financial benefit for their project. In fact, in some cases, their immediate costs may be higher. Externality theory teaches that public goods are best paid for by public works and not by individuals.

For client/server to work, a shared public architecture is necessitated. Such an architecture is a public good. Public goods should be funded by the corporate entity and not directly allocated to each project. The cost of infrastructure should not be front loaded to new client/server projects but priced to each on a reasonable amortization basis.

5. Most MPS cost analysis use some form of return on investment, payback, internal rate of return, net present value or simple cost/benefits of moving to client/server. As normally presented they are analytically correct but strategically sterile. It is becoming recognized that these methods do not routinely take into account the future option values that a client/server investment provides. It is therefore necessary to amend these methods to assign future option values to the client/server systems. Having built the system with a maneuverable client/server architecture, what is it worth now to have that increased flexibility later? By taking into full account the turbulence of our times and allocating dollar benefits to being able to deal with that turbulence, we more fairly assign benefits to the client/server solution. We must remember that all our I/T investments are being made under a condition of increasing uncertainty. There is value that should be recognized in investments that are more easily altered to deal with a chaotic future. We must recognize that different types of investments have different effects on the ability of the business to make future investments. Appropriate cost benefits must be allocated to those current investments that provide for quicker and more cost efficient future investment options.

6. The issue of *hidden costs* is a double-edged sword. As intended by mainframe proponents, they are referring to labor costs incurred by C/S users as they perform OA&M functions such as installations, backup, trouble shooting, etc. Hidden costs, however, also has a formal meaning in the economic theory of capital. In that case, hidden costs designates the lost opportunity (the penalty) that occurs when a company borrows money in capital markets at one rate (say 9%) and, by virtue of its invest-

ments, grows at a rate less than the borrow rate (say it grows at 5% resulting in a hidden cost of opportunity lost of 4%).

What has been the hidden cost of mainframe computing? How much opportunity has been lost to the business because it was unable to maneuver? How much revenue has been lost, though hidden, because the information technology systems couldn't respond in a timely manner? So if we are going to address the hidden costs of CSC, we should also address the hidden costs of mainframe computing and the magnitude of those mainframe hidden costs are embodied in Figures 3.6 to 3.12.

We now have a complete understanding of how the economics of CSC work.

HOW SHOULD C/S BE COSTED?

We would therefore assert that the proper way to cost C/S applications is as follows:

1. Design an overall I/T architecture that for a given family of applications, A, has a high degree of potential resource sharing, S. Choose I/T objects of size U to balance C_u and C_m.
2. Cost out moving the applications to this shared architecture with the understanding and strategic intent that each additional application takes maximum advantage of services that have been provided by the previously completed applications.
3. Take into account the S curve effect on labor-intensive activities. Each year, the entrepreneurial cycle will reduce your labor costs. It will assuredly reduce your labor costs because the reduction of labor costs has always been the primary target of automation and that is where profits are to be made for vendors.
4. Demonstrate the effect of changes on the cost structure. Since the architecture is C/S, what is the effect of adding one additional transaction that in C/S might only require upgrading a single server but will require a whole new mainframe for the host-centered architecture? This new upgraded mainframe will, of course, have resources that are not needed but need to be paid for.
5. Demonstrate the effect of building an unanticipated additional application. With so many reusable services in place, how will

the cost of responding to new business opportunities compare with the mainframe alternative?

6. Include in the benefit part of the cost/benefit calculations, the option value that the client/server architecture provides to the business. Having built this application in the more maneuverable client/server architecture, what is it worth to you now to know that you have untapped adaptability to deal with future business unknowns?

7. Do not charge the full cost of infrastructure (particularly network) to the application. Since infrastructure is a public good, it should be charged at a fair amortized rate.

8. Take into account the alleviation of the hidden costs of mainframe computing. As client/server computing alleviates the traditional mainframe failings, what is it worth to you that management will no longer have to focus on the same set of issues that have hoarded its attention for the last 15 years?

In this way, while you cost host-centered computing in a way consistent with its monolithic nature, you cost C/S in a way consistent with its sharing nature. What could be fairer?

THE MPS COST STUDIES

With our preparation completed, we can now analyze the MPS cost studies that allegedly *proved*, without question, that mainframe computing was cheaper than CSC. In Chapter 1, when I quoted the MPS assertions, I did not explicitly attribute the statements. The reason was that I do not wish to engage in any personal debates or attacks; my disagreement is with the general assertions and the quotes served but for examples. The same is true here. I will refute the MPS cost studies as a unified collection and not individually.

The MPS cost studies that assert that C/S computing is more expensive than host-centered computing do not prove that at all for the following reasons:

1. They use economies of scale as the economic framework for costing client/server rather than economies of sharing.

2. They do not take into account the effect of the entrepreneurial cycle in reducing labor costs and providing rich OA&M.

3. They do not rearchitect the applications into an architecture with a high A and a high S.
4. They do not take into account any changes or maneuverability during the costing period. They never show the effect of the next marginal change that will cause a massive cost increase for the host-centered architecture because the unit of scalability is so large. They assume a stable business environment when, in reality, the business environment is best characterized as exploding turbulence.
5. They often compare apples with oranges. The often-quoted study that asserts the 14.3 to 1 cost disadvantage for C/S states that the transactions of the study samples are "qualitatively different" (i.e., the mainframe examples were for transaction systems and the C/S systems were departmental and personal). The cost comparison is admittedly meaningless, yet it is routinely quoted as scientific proof.[3]
6. They assume that you are getting equal-value propositions. This is not true. As we presented in Chapter 3, C/S has a vastly superior value proposition. Even if C/S were more expensive (it is not), its ratio of value proposition to cost would still exceed that of mainframe computing.
7. Some of the studies complain that the C/S solutions are more expensive because they have richer functionality and are changed more rapidly and often to respond to customer requests. This is a most interesting criticism.
8. They do not take into account the cost of delivering equal functionality from a mainframe that is delivered from an intelligent client. Can advanced user interfaces, GUI, voice recognition, scanning, virtual reality, and so on be offered at any price from a host environment? They ignore the convergence of interactive multimedia.

These cost studies are conceptually and methodologically flawed. They do not prove what they assert. To the contrary, when you cost out C/S as we have suggested and take into account the value proposition, the results will be extraordinarily favorable to C/S.

SUMMARY

The following quote from an MPS enthusiast defined the point of contention addressed in this chapter:

> The bloated costs of client/server computing are becoming so obvious that they can no longer be ignored. C/S is an extravagant/expensive solution that offers nothing beyond some trendy intangibles and a negative return on investment.

Do you accept that? I certainly do not and have tried in this chapter to share with you my rationale for believing that C/S is not only cheaper but a superior value proposition as well.

The core of our argument was as follows:

- The economics of CSC are driven by economies of sharing.
- The entrepreneurial cycle is voraciously addressing any and all points of labor intensity.
- The cost studies of the MPS are conceptually and methodologically flawed.
- C/S must be costed using a different methodology that emphasizes sharing.
- The value proposition of C/S is dramatically superior to mainframe computing and yields a value proposition/cost ratio that is dramatically superior to mainframe computing.

Another MPS partisan said "If customers are anticipating saving money with C/S, *they are nuts.*" Who is nuts, if anyone, is subject to intense debate.

EPILOGUE

The evidence has been presented. While this evidence is heretical to the sensibilities of some traditional mainframe enthusiasts, the argument is well reasoned and provides a novel approach appropriate for technology on a different S curve. The calumny against CSC has been rebutted. The defense rests. The verdict resides, as it must, not with gurus, pundits, market researchers, oracles, soothsayers, necromancers, academics, or authors, but with you, the marketplace. I believe the votes that you freely cast every day when your spend your I/T dollars tell us exactly what you believe.

My research tells me that the S curve substitution is accelerating and that the one-two punch of flexibility and cost advantage is too much to ignore regardless of your historical affection for mainframe computing. In the year 2000, the companies at the frontier of I/T efficiency will be there not because of economies of scale but because of economies of sharing. In the year 2000, the companies at the leading edge of business success will be those who best exploit CSC. Where will you be?

NOTES

1. The material in this section on cost curves is based on the work of Professor Levent Orman of the Graduate School of Management at Cornell University. Please see "Information Cost as a Determinant of System Architecture," Levent Orman, *Information and Software Technology,* 1994, 36 (3) for the original article. I would like to express my thanks to Professor Orman for his help and permission in using this material. My presentation is a highly simplified summary of his material, and I strongly recommend that you read the original to fully understand the many details that I ignored for simplicity.

2. Obviously mainframes, through interrupts and virtual memory, were very adept at sharing MIPS and memory. What we want to share, however, are business objects (databases, application logic, etc.) that are much more valuable.

3. For example, an article entitled "Price/Performance and Manageability Maintain the Mainframe Niche," *Client/Server Computing,* July 1995, builds its cost argument on the meaningless 14.3 to 1 cost comparison.

5

Data Architecture, Data Placement, and a Distributed Database in a Client/Server Environment

The purpose of this chapter is to provide a comprehensive analysis of the issues surrounding the building of a distributed data environment for a business. Two primary and relentless trends have made it highly desirable to distribute data across the enterprise:

- *Business Reengineering:* There is an intense desire to reengineer business processes to infuse them with speed, agility, customer focus, value added, and/or to minimize cost. Business reengineers wish to move data to where it will optimize the business process but not jeopardize data integrity, availability, and accessibility.
- *Client/Server Computing:* Distributed processing, in a myriad of forms but predominately the client/server architecture, is becoming the dominant information technology processing architecture. Client/server permits the business to distribute presentation, function, and data layers of business applications to where they make the most business sense. Client/server has become highly desirable and possible due to changing economies of information technologies and the desire to empower workers.

The two trends are quite complementary and synergistic (Figure 5.1). Business reengineering requires client/server computing to provide a robust platform upon which to reengineer applications,

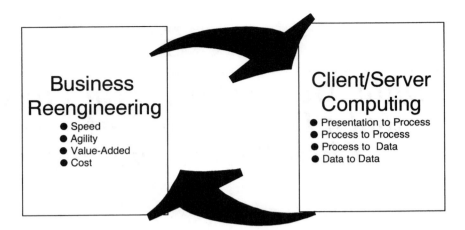

Business Reengineering
- Speed
- Agility
- Value-Added
- Cost

Client/Server Computing
- Presentation to Process
- Process to Process
- Process to Data
- Data to Data

Figure 5.1   **Business reengineering and client/server computing. Each promotes the other.**

and the need for client/server is made compelling and its desirability enhanced by the urge to reengineer.

The most valuable information technology asset to a business is its data. For most of the history of commercial data processing, the data asset has been managed within host-centric mainframe computing architectures. Business reengineering coupled with client/server computing makes it desirable to move data to the location in the business that makes the most business sense but maintains data integrity, availability, and accessibility. A new challenge then emerges: How is that to be done?

This chapter develops a logical but pragmatic taxonomy of the issues involved in creating a distributed data architecture, choosing data placement, and designing distributed databases in support of business reengineering with client/server technology. Distributed data architecture and databases will demand that new information technology engineering skills be developed. It will be well worth the effort because those businesses that master distributing data within a client/server environment will have the basis for building far superior business processes and will therefore accomplish the most coveted of all business goals; they will be able to build and sustain *advantage*.

THE STRATEGIC BUSINESS NEED FOR DISTRIBUTED DATA

With distributed database technology, users are presented with a global schema that hides the underlying locations and structure of the data and databases. The data assets can therefore be changed, moved, or replicated, as required, to quickly respond to the business environmental diversity without causing disruption. The data assets remain logically stable while physically in motion. They can be positioned where it makes the most architectural sense now but be reconfigured later in response to changing times and circumstances. Data architecture takes on the quality of being "temporary" by design as opposed to being "fixed." It takes on the quality of being fluid instead of being solid.

The strategic significance of a distributed database is as follows:

- Client/server computing with its primary application, a distributed database offers extraordinary diversity in the management of the data assets. The data assets become formless like water; they can be moved, replicated, or changed to quickly cope with the shifting business diversity but maintain a constant transparent interface to the nonimpacted user community. Nondisruptive change with alacrity can take place.
- It will permit the business in a world of increasing torrid global competition to *maneuver* with unparalleled swiftness.
- Data is the primary reusable service in a client/server environment. If economies of sharing are to be accomplished, data must be positioned as a high reuse service. The two great benefits of CSC, flexibility and cost advantage, cannot be achieved unless the corporation's data is properly managed.

In summary, what the business strategically demands of its I/T assets is incredible and cost-effective flexibility to enable dramatic maneuverability against a value chain background characterized by constantly shifting needs for information exchange between the participants (Figure 2.17). Distributed databases offer the means to make the data assets phenomenally responsive to diversity. The mission and challenge to the I/T organization is to implement a distributed database to provide the maximum flexibility at the minimum cost. A distributed database is of strategic interest not just because it will save money, improve performance, or improve reliability (all very good, but not enough), but because it is the means to optimize the range in a reach, range, and maneuver I/T architecture (Figure 3.15).

SCOPE AND DEFINITIONS

The issues surrounding the distribution of data in a client/server environment are numerous. This chapter focuses only on the direct "data" issues and not on the supporting/enabling issues. In designing a distributed database environment, it is obvious that the processing platforms and operating systems selected and the communications/networking choices made are also critically important. The selected set of database mangers must work on/with them in the desired manner. We will ignore them in this essay but with the realization that in implementing a distributed database environment, it is necessary to either constrain your database design choices by a given set of platforms, operating systems, and communication capabilities, or validate and choose a set of platforms, operating systems, and communication capabilities in parallel with the distributed database design effort. In the first case, distributed database design must be done within the limitations of a given environment. In the latter case, distributed database design drives (or is a coequal determinant of) the other factors. The methodology presented in this chapter works with both situations. Though we won't explicitly do it, one must imagine the design process taking place with these environmental issues in the background and periodically constraining or being decided by the distributed database design.

The methodology will also make no assumptions about the homogeneity or heterogeneity of the selected database managers. The database manager(s) to be used may be a given or it may be a design choice. The database mangers may be homogeneous or heterogeneous. By *homogeneous* we mean the same database manager is present on all participating database nodes. In a strict sense, homogeneous could mean the exact same release level on all nodes. We will interpret homogeneous to mean a set of database mangers from a vendor, at the same release level or not, supporting the same (relational) data model, which have been designed to work together to deliver distributed database functionality. Heterogeneity means that the database managers are from different vendors and, possibly, the data models supported by the differing database mangers are also dissimilar (i.e., rather then all the databases being a relational variant, some are hierarchical, network, object, or flat files). Combining this with the previous discussion, the most difficult design case is different data model heterogeneous databases running on different platforms with different operating systems communicating though different communication protocols. We are limiting our scope to the heterogeneous database case only.

The methodology presented herein will work equally well with homogeneous or heterogeneous database managers. The design process will eliminate those combinations of homogeneous or heterogeneous managers that cannot deliver the required functionality. It is obvious that the more sophisticated functionality can only be delivered by a carefully designed homogenous environment.

While there are endless variants, there are two primary multidatabase situations. The first, which we call a *distributed database,* involves the top-down explicit design of a set of distributed databases to work together across a network. In working together, they assure integrity, coherency, access transparency, replicability, recovery, and so forth per our top-down design choices. The presenting design problem is what do you want the distributed database to do. In the second case, which we call a *federated database,* we are presented with a set of databases (homogeneous or not, same data model or not) on which we wish to retroactively impose a logical global schema to make them operate as a distributed database; it is a bottom-up design problem. The presenting design problem here is a question of what you can do with the variety you've been given. This chapter deals with the first situation, which is common in business reengineering.

DEFINITIONS

The following definitions are given for certain critical concepts:

- *Database:* A collection of information objects with integrity constraints. Information objects include data elements, tables, indexes, views, schemas, referential integrity rules, access rules, and so on. Information objects may take many forms such as text, sound, image, video, and graphics, i.e., information convergence.

- *Distributed Database:* A collection of databases that function as a unified whole. Through the global schema, users see a single logical database that is, in reality, a set of distinct physical databases. Though each physical database functions as a complete individual database, the distributed database functionality ensures that integrity, coherency, recoverability, and so on can be accomplished across the databases as though they were physically one.
- *Global Schema:* A schema that gives a logical global view of all the databases comprising the distributed database. Each database also has a local schema that defines its resident data for itself. Data access though the global schema permits location transparency, since the requester has no notion of where the physical data is stored. Users are provided with a global schema consistent with their access rights.
- *Replication:* A copy of an information object. The copy may be exactly the same (i.e., an exact copy of a table) or it may be different (i.e., only a few data elements from a table are duplicated). A replicated table may be stored in a different storage structure than the original table. A master copy is designated the copy of record. When replicated copies are the same value as the master copy, they are said to be in a state of *coherence;* when they are not, they are said to be in a state of *incoherence.*
- *Transaction:* A sequence of operations (add, modify, delete, select) that potentially modify the state of a database. In database processing, transactions are generally sandwiched by a *start transaction* statement and end with either a *commit* or an *abort* statement. Transactions are characterized by four basic properties known collectively as the ACID properties:

  - *Atomicity:* A transaction either commits, in which case all the effects of the transaction are applied against the database, or it aborts, in which case none of the transactions is applied against the database.
  - *Consistency:* The transaction moves the database from one valid state to another valid state.
  - *Isolation:* The property that guarantees that the effect of concurrently executing transaction is equivalent to executing the transactions in serial order.
  - *Durability:* The property of persistence (that once a transaction is committed, its effects will survive system crashes or other failures).

- *Two-Phase Commit:* A protocol between member databases of a distributed database that ensures transaction ACIDity when a transaction must update across multiple physical databases.

ROAD MAP

The remainder of this chapter provides a presentation of the logical steps necessary to design, implement, operate, and evolve a distributed database environment. The following topics will be analyzed:

- *The Mainframe Legacy Data Architecture.* This section briefly reviews the traditional mainframe database environment and analyze its strengths and weaknesses.
- *Data Architecture.* This section develops the argument that the best data architecture for a business is a dual database architecture in which one set of databases, subject databases, are used to run the business and a separate set of databases, decision support databases (a.k.a. data warehouse databases), are used to analyze the business.
- *Database Partition and Replication Design.* This section analyzes the alternative partitioning choices available to the distributed database designer. It also analyzes the types of replication available and the advantages and disadvantages of each.
- *Individual Database Design.* Each database within the distributed database environment is a complete functional database and needs to be individually designed. This section analyzes the steps required to do individual database design.
- *Batch Processing.* This section analyzes additional distributed database design issues required to support batch processing
- *Transaction Monitors.* This section analyzes the need to decide whether the distributed database environment should make use of a distributed transaction monitor.
- *Life-Cycle Distributed Database Maintenance.* This section analyzes the types of changes that may be made to a distributed database environment over its life cycle.
- *Operations, Administration and Maintenance (OA&M).* This section analyzes the required production operations capabilities that are required to manage the production use of a distributed database.

- *Modeling.* This section analyzes the types of modeling and prototyping required to choose between candidate designs.
- *Risk Assessment.* This section analyzes the need for a running risk assessment throughout the entire design process.
- *Implications.* This section presents a set of implications on the design of the overall I/T environment to effectively deal with the new distributed database reality.

While the methodology may be presented as a sequential linear process, in practice it is best to think of it as a forward spiral with periodic iteration. Each design issue temporarily will take front stage in the design process, but all issues must be kept in mind regardless of which one is currently at stage front. Though we are not including the issues of platforms, operating systems, and communications in this chapter (per our previous scope definition), one would include them in the same manner as all other design issues. Figure 5.2 illustrates the relative prominence of the different design issues throughout the development and design process.

Given the limitlessness of possible designs, it is helpful to view the process as the development of a set of alternative distributed database scenarios that are being continually tested, altered, and refined as the different design issues are applied against them. As you will see, a final engineering-based decision will most likely require the building of simulation and volume models to judge the comparative efficacy of the final candidate scenarios.

The design, development, implementation, operation, and evolution of a distributed database environment is a sophisticated engineering problem. While it is challenging, with the use of a structured engineering methodology, it is solvable. Though some will wish to refrain from the challenge, we should always remember why we are doing this. The strategic requirement for I/T is to overlay flexibility on business diversity. Since the set of possible distributed database designs is inexhaustible, distributed database technology exactly meets the needs of the business to have I/T endlessly reconfigure itself to meet the constantly changing information diversity needs of the business. This is why distributed database design is worth the challenge and why those businesses that can overlay distributed database flexibility on business environmental diversity will have a clear superiority in meeting the constantly shifting needs of the marketplace.

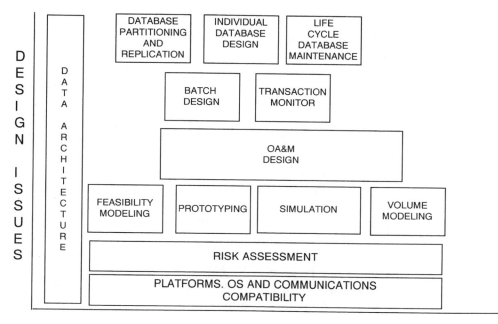

T I M E

Figure 5.2   Distributed database design issues. Different design issues take on interim prominence as the distributed database design progresses.

THE MAINFRAME LEGACY DATA ARCHITECTURE

The history of data architecture is, for the most part, the history of centralized data management. Though there are always exceptions, data architecture naturally reflected the historically dominant mainframe host-centric processing paradigm. The database environment could be described as follows:

- Independent databases were developed to reflect the needs of a specific application or a family of related applications. These databases were primarily either file systems, hierarchical databases, network databases, inverted key databases, or, more recently, relational databases.
- There was no pretense that the databases were designed segments of a single logical integrated database. They were fully functional standalone databases that managed the specific data for the owning applications.

- Users had to sign onto each system and move themselves between them. There was no transparency of data location.
- Coherence was maintained between databases by periodic batch extracts and snapshots from the database that was designated the "copy of record" to the other databases. In some cases, message switching systems such as multiple-system coupling (MSC) and intersystem coupling (ISC) were used to route transactions between database managers and perform interactive coherence. In the worst cases, different and asynchronous update streams were used to update the same data elements in different databases, causing permanent incoherence.
- Production databases (transaction processing) did not permit ad hoc query or decision support applications to be run against them. Extracts were periodically taken and loaded onto report databases like FOCUS or RAMIS in a time-shared environment (i.e., the VM operating system, where users were free to do their ad hoc reporting and analysis).
- If the organization was well run, data administration assured that data element definitions were consistent across databases. More often then not, data administration was not well run and spaghetti-like batch interfaces were required to "clean and reformat" data as it moved between applications and databases.
- The databases were often dispersed. There would be multiple databases that coexisted independently on the same mainframe processor, on different processors in the same data center, or on different processors in different data centers. Updating to the centralized databases normally took place in two styles:

  - *On-line Transaction Processing:* Dispersed users sitting at "dumb" terminals invoked transaction processing (often COBOL or 4th GL) programs that, running under a transaction monitor (IMS-DC or CICS), would access and update the database. Transactions had the character of being very short-lived and were often designed with the notion of a maximum "unit of work" to ensure performance.
  - *Batch Processing:* Batches of transactions were gathered and applied as a group against the database. The on-line system was normally "down" during the batch execution window.

- Database administration and operations was handled by a centralized and professional I/T staff members in the data center environment.
- A centralized disaster recovery plan existed to ensure the continuance of operations in the event of a failure.

This environment offered the following advantages:

- There was experienced and professional management of the data resource.
- There was tight control of the data resource.
- There was tight security of the data resource.
- The database existed as a single logical and physical entity. It was conceptually easy for people to understand where the data was and to perform the necessary OA&M functions against it. Centralized databases were and remain appropriate for situations where

  1. There is frequent updating by widely dispersed users without any recognizable locality of reference.
  2. The transaction mix continually accesses the database both vertically and horizontally.
  3. All the users require the up-to-the-minute versions of the data and replication techniques are inadequate.

As was argued previously, the strategic problem confronting the business is the overlaying of I/T flexibility on accelerating business environmental diversity. Distributed database management is desired because it offers an extraordinarily flexible response to this demand. If a proper distributed database environment is built with data transparency to the users, the business is then free to continually reorganize and reoptimize its data environment in harmony with the changing environmental diversity but can maintain a transparent interface to the user community.

The decision to move to a distributed database environment from the legacy host-centric environment is therefore motivated by the following:

- Most users require access to multiple databases. The creation of a global schema that provides transparent access makes the user's database independent while providing flexibility for the business to move data and databases as required by the shifting environmental diversity.

- Some databases and/or transaction rates exceed the management limits of conventional information technology. Partitioning and replication are the only design alternatives for managing the data or transaction volumes.
- By dispersing the database segment and replication copies, improvements in availability, performance, reliability, security, and cost are often obtainable.
- The built-in replication capabilities of distributed database managers provide an excellent mechanism to move data from the production databases to the decision support databases in an orderly and controlled manner.

It is important to recognize that the historical centralized database management is simply the null case of a distributed database environment. This is the heart of the issue of I/T flexibility. A distributed database environment can do all that a centralized database management, the most simple reduction design, can do, but it can also do much, much more. It is this ability to do much, much more in response to the business environmental diversity that makes a distributed database a business imperative. With the historical mainframe data architecture, "one size" did fit all. With a distributed database architecture, the business is positioned to endlessly reconfigure its data resources to be in evolving harmony with the dynamic environmental diversity. In this way, through distributed database technology, I/T responds to the strategic needs of the business for maneuverability from its I/T data assets and achieves a superior state of strategic alignment between I/T and the business.

DATA ARCHITECTURE[1]

The business practices of the enterprise are automated in the form of business applications that collectively compose the business systems portfolio. Companies have innumerable processes requiring I/T capability. Typical applications would include order realization, customer service, contract administration, product development, benefits administration, staffing, budget development and monitoring, and information sharing (e-mail, conferencing, team support, etc.). The list is endless.

As illustrated in Figure 5.3, the business practices can generally be partitioned into two broad classifications:

- *The Business Applications:* Those business applications that operationally "run" the business on a daily, weekly, monthly, and so on basis. When they cease to run, the business literally stops operating.
- *The About the Business Applications:* Those applications that analyze the business. They aid in interpreting what has occurred and in deciding prudent actions for the future. When they cease to run, there is no immediately obvious business failure, but their utility is critical to the long-term competitiveness of the enterprise.

"The Business Applications" are often called On-Line Transaction Processing Systems (OLTP) or Operations Support Systems (OSS) and have the following general attributes:

1. They are "heavy-duty" production transaction record-keeping systems that directly support the execution of a business practice.

BUSINESS PRACTICES							
THE BUSINESS APPLICATIONS			THE ABOUT THE BUSINESS APPLICATIONS				
OLTP	OSS	TIME-SHARED	MODELING	INFOR-MATION RETRIEVAL	AD-HOC REPORTING	DECISION SUPPORT	INFORMA-TION SHARING

Figure 5.3 The application portfolio. Business applications can be divided into those that run the business and those that analyze the business. (Source: *Implementing Client/Server Computing,* Bernard H. Boar, McGraw-Hill, 1993.)

2. They may have to provide 24-hour by 7-day service and have carefully managed outage periods.
3. Database integrity and availability are crucial. The database must be recoverable from a failure within a guaranteed restoration period.
4. They are performance measurable in terms of transactions/(sub)second and/or user response time [x% of the transactions must respond in less than y (sub)seconds].
5. They are structured applications with both predefined transactions and predefined transaction flows. The execution paths are predictable.
6. The database schemas are quite complex in terms of number of entities and number of interentity relationships. The interentity relationships impose multiple dependency, referential integrity, and validation requirements on the system.
7. Elaborate editing of input transactions is required to ensure and maintain database quality.
8. Security of access is important.
9. Sophisticated dialogue management is required.
10. There is a strong concern for user ergonomics to maximize productivity.
11. They are often large applications by the metrics of database size, total number of users, total number of concurrent users, and types of transactions.
12. There is extensive off-prime time batch updating and reporting that must be completed within a tight batch window.

The payoff advantage from these types of applications is business performance. Consequently, they will often contain exception monitoring subsystems used to advise management when an abnormal situation has occurred or an undesirable pattern is developing.

The "About the Business Applications" are often called Information Center Applications (decision support, modeling, information retrieval, ad hoc reporting/analysis, what-if, data warehouses, etc.). This class of applications are retrieval/analysis/report/information-sharing oriented. The data sources are often triggered extracts from OLTP or OSS applications or public information services. These applications have the following attributes:

1. Static (low update) databases.
2. Periodic refreshing of the database from the source OLTP or OSS application.

3. Extended time accumulation of data.
4. Simple restore/recovery.
5. Facilities to enable the "canning" of repetitive user requests.
6. Flexible import/export facilities.
7. They enable information sharing.
8. An analyst workbench that may include graphics tools, report writers, statistical modeling tools, spreadsheets, simulators, query languages, word processors, desktop publishing, project management software, artificial intelligent tools, data mining tools, information discovery tools, application development tools, and information exchange tools.

The payoff from this class of applications is better knowledge about the business and the development of future business strategies.

Applications are often continuous in capability, and their functionality may not be discrete. Though an application will normally naturally migrate to one classification as its primary definer, it may have subsystems that are more aligned to the other type. Both the business applications and the about the business applications with all their endless variations are built on top of a data architecture and a processing architecture that jointly compose the I/T architecture for the business.

DATA ARCHITECTURE

Business applications are performed by programs that collect, create, modify, retrieve, and delete data and programs that use, analyze, summarize, extract, and/or in other ways manipulate data. Data is the common thread that ties together the extensive corporate application portfolio. Data, as it is transformed into information as it flows between users, can provide current advantage in the form of superior operational systems and future advantage in the form of superior analysis for planning. How the data asset is positioned is of vital long-term importance to the health of the enterprise.

Increasingly, corporations are recognizing that the purposeful management and leveraging of the corporate data asset must take on increased attention in the 1990s. In the 1970s, management attention was focused on hardware cost. During the 1980s, management's attention shifted to software as both a growing element of the I/T cost structure and the source of advantageous applications. In the 1990s, management will increasingly focus on data exploitation as the path to improved customer service, cooperation with suppliers, and the creation of new barriers for competitors.

Data engineering theory (data engineering is the discipline that studies how to model, analyze, and design data for maximum utility) indicates that there are four generic data environments on which to build business applications. For a variety of technical and architectural reason they are not equally advantageous. Figure 5.4 illustrates the four options and can be explained as follows:

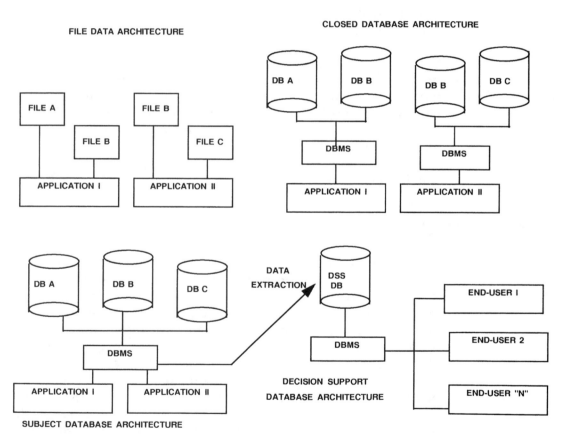

Figure 5.4   Data architecture. There are four ways to organize an organization's data. (Source: *Implementing Client/Server Computing,* **Bernard H. Boar, McGraw-Hill, 1993.)**

1. *Dedicated File Architecture:* Each application has a set of privately designed files. The data structure is tightly embedded with the application, and the data files are owned by the application.

2. *Closed Database Architecture:* A database management system (DBMS) is used to provide technological advantage over file systems (exemplary advantages are views, security, atomicity, locking, recovery, etc.) but distinct, separate, and independent databases are still designed for each application. The DBMS is used as a private and powerful file system with the data remaining the proprietary property of the application. As is true with the dedicated file architecture, there is a high degree of data redundancy and frequently poor data administration. Spaghettilike interfaces move data between the closed databases. Since these interfaces often have to convert, edit, and/or restructure data as it moves between proprietary definitions, they are often called "data scrubbers" or translators. Data scrubbers do not add value; they compensate for inadequate data administration.

3. *Subject Database Architecture:* Data is analyzed, modeled, structured, and stored based on its own internal attributes, independent of any specific application. Data is administered as a shareable resource through a data administration function that owns the data for all potential users. Extensive sharing of data occurs through application sensitive views. Subject databases run the day-to-day operations of the enterprise.

4. *Decision Support Database Architecture:* Databases are constructed for quick searching retrieval, ad hoc queries, and ease of use. The data is normally a periodic extract from a subject database or pubic information service. To minimize the number of extracts and to ensure time/content consistent data, data is shared at the corporate, departmental, and local levels, not extracted per user. Data definitions are maintained in synchronization with the source databases to ensure the ability to interrelate data from multiple subject database extracts without the need to resort to "data scrubbers." Decision support databases are used to analyze the enterprise.

The recommended data architecture is a mixture of the subject database and decision support database environments: subject databases to support the business applications and decision support databases to enable the about the business applications. This dual database architecture is most advantageous for the following reasons:

- It maximizes data quality.
- It maximizes data accessibility.
- It maximizes data sharing.
- It eliminates unplanned-for data redundancy.
- It simplifies interapplication interaction.
- It assures data standardization.
- It maximizes application life-cycle productivity.
- It accelerates the development of new applications that can reuse the in-place data resource.
- It enables the creation of centers of excellence in data management to protect the data asset.

Figure 5.5 illustrates what the optimum data architecture would look like. It merges the subject database and decision support database environments together.

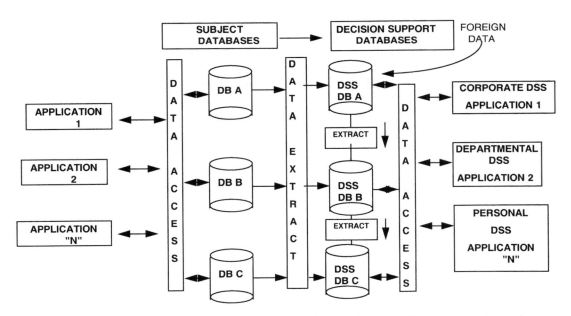

Figure 5.5   **Optimum data architecture. The optimum data architecture consists of a family of subject databases to run the business and a family of coupled decision support databases to analyze the business. (Source:** *Implementing Client/Server Computing,* **Bernard H. Boar, McGraw-Hill, 1993.)**

Some data architects would prefer a single database environment where both OLTP and decision support needs are fulfilled concurrently against a single database and thereby eliminate duplication and extract altogether. It is our assessment that the two user communities have fundamentally different and incompatible requirements that preclude this ideal option. Table 5.1 summarizes the major points of conflict. These dichotomies present a formidable barrier to a single database environment.

When routine access is given to operational databases by decision support users, experience suggests the following major problems occur:

1. *Performance:* The unpredictable nature of the ad hoc queries disrupts the requirement of predictable response time for operational systems. Predictable and guaranteed performance cannot be engineered into the system design if the transactions are not predictable.

Table 5.1
Subject Database and Decision Support Database Dichotomies.

Operational Environment: Subject Databases— The Business Applications	Decision Support Environment: Decision Support Databases— The About the Business Applications
Stores very detailed data	Stores detailed and/or summarized data
Stores entire subject database	Stores only data of interest
Requires to the last transaction accuracy	Requires "as of" accuracy
Disciplined and highly structured planned transactions	Unstructured and ad hoc transactions
Optimized for performance, efficiency, and availability	Optimized for flexibility and ease of use
Maintains rigorous data structures	Supports dynamic data structures
Runs the business	Analyzes the business
Emphasizes needs of all potential users	Emphasizes needs of each user
Short-running and engineered transactions	Potentially long-running and dynamically defined transactions

The demands on each type of database are fundamentally different. (Source: *Implementing Client/Server Computing,* Bernard H. Boar, McGraw-Hill, 1993.)

2. *Data Retention:* The decision support applications often require retention of data longer, for cumulative analysis, than the operational systems, which only need it for the active business practice cycle. The growth in the size of the database can negatively impact performance, integrity, and the ability to meet any recoverability time constraints.
3. *Logical Reasoning:* Since the database is dynamically changing with each transaction, information queries are not repeatable and chained queries do not necessarily operate on the same set of data. Deductive reasoning against a stable data store is not feasible. A temporal database that maintains a time view of the data could resolve this problem but creates a new set of issues unrelated to the pressing operational needs.

We may summarize our views on data architecture as follows:

- There are four generic ways to design and organize the corporation's data asset.
- They are not equal.
- A combination of the subject database and decision support database environments is most advantageous. This is called a dual database environment.
- A single database environment from which both operational and decision support requirements are met is desirable but plagued by many practical problems that make it infeasible.

It is important to remember that the databases in Figure 5.5 are logical subject and decision support databases. Their physical design in terms of partitioning and replication is at the discretion of the database implementation design team. Distributed database technology offers the opportunity to implement a robust dual database environment that optimizes the competing demands for integrity, coherence, performance, availability, and cost. In other words, a distributed database environment offers a more flexible I/T capability to deliver a dual database environment that can continually evolve with the shifting environmental business diversity.

DATABASE PARTITION AND REPLICATION DESIGN

Distributed database design is the decomposition of "a" logical database into a set of logical databases that will be converted into physical databases that operate both as individual databases and as a unified whole. The process consists of seven steps:

1. Business Analysis

Using any of a variety of business analysis techniques such as structured analysis, object oriented analysis, or process modeling, a broad and deep understanding of the business needs that will be required of the subject database and/or decision support database is developed.

2. Logical Data Model

A normalized logical data model of the database (a single database) is developed. In support of this model are the following types of critical design items:

- Data entity volumes: the startup and annual growth rates for each data entity (table).
- Rules of referential integrity across the data entities.
- The types of transactions that will be applied against the database.
- Normal transaction volumes and peak volumes.
- The topology (geographical dispersion) of the updaters of the database.
- The topology (geographical dispersion) of the users of the database.
- The interactive and batch mix of transactions.
- The required performance of each transaction.
- The required availability of the overall system and logical sub-grouping of transactions.
- The batch window (or if 24-hour transaction availability is required).
- The target cost per transaction.
- Security requirements.

The purpose of this information is to try to get a clear understanding of the volatility of the database entities, the volume of updates, the geographic sources of the updates, and the locality of reference of the updates. Using this information one can make the partitioning decisions that will be described in the next two steps. Figure 5.6 can provide assistance in organizing the transaction data.

User Group and Geography	Transactions and Mode (Batch/On-line)	Transaction Attributes	Transaction Values
User Group 1 at Site A	Transaction A	Normal Volume Peak Volume Performance Availability Security Data Locality of Reference	
	Transaction B	Normal Volume Peak Volume Etc.	

Figure 5.6 Organizing transaction data. The attributes of each transaction can be organized using a form such as this.

3. Database Partitioning

Using the information from step 2, there are three basic ways in which the logical database can be partitioned. Each partition will represent a future physical instance of the distributed database, and a decision will have to be made as to the specific geographical placement of the partition. The partitions of a distributed database have to maintain integrity as though they were logically one (i.e., transactions have to pass the ACID test). In this environment, this is done through use of a two-phase commit protocol. The two-phase commit protocol assures that even though the partitions are physically separate, they logically maintain transaction integrity (i.e., ACIDity). The partitioning design must remember that there is significant overhead for two-phase commit processing and that partitioning design must take two-phase processing into account. One is confronted with a dilemma that must be balanced and resolved. At one end, we would like to maximize distribution to bring data as close to users as possible, but, at the other end, increasing distribution will increase the two-phase commit over-head, which can drastically negatively effect performance.

The following three partitioning design alternatives are available.

a. *Horizontal Partitioning* (Figure 5.7)

Database records (relations) are segmented and collocated by a defining key. This requires that a global identifier be associated with multiple database records and that the global identifier be the essential key of those records. A typical horizontal partition would be to collocate all record types for an employee.

Horizontal partitioning is a natural way to segment that is often in harmony with the way transactions are structured, and user administration of the database can often be partitioned in parallel to support this structure, enabling a horizontal data-

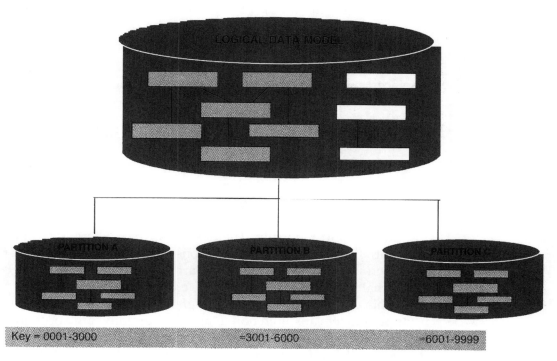

Figure 5.7 **Horizontal database partitioning. The database is partitioned horizontally by key values.**

base partition to service a horizontal group of users. This type of partitioning also supports referential integrity, since all the records for the global identifier are in one place.

The following key issues need to be considered:

   i. How many horizontal segments should there be and what would be the typical size of a grouping?

   ii. How will transactions that are entity type intensive be handled? Recall that in a horizontal partitioning, all the instances of an entity type are dispersed across the horizontal partitions. This is especially a concern for batch reporting and entity intensive updating.

   iii. What would be involved to either resize partitions (load balancing) or add new entity types once the database is in production. The ability to resize is necessary to scale the partitions as the volume of records grows (i.e., the way to deal with growth in database size or transaction volumes is to create more partitions that can be independently updated). The ability to add new entity types is necessary to be able to evolve the database as business diversity adds demands.

The final issue with a horizontal partition is its physical placement. This is a function of analyzing the locality of reference and frequency of update from step 2.

b. *Vertical Partitioning* (Figure 5.8)

Database records (relations) are segmented and collocated by entity types. The partition exactly mirrors the notion of a subject database with a set of related entity types being the factor of collocation. In this design, it is relatively easy to add new entity types as new partitions. The design also makes clear where data entities exist and is ideally suited for functional updating and reporting. The design is weak where horizontal partitioning is strong. Transactions that are global identifier driven will have to cross many partitions to complete, and referential integrity will also involve crossing many partitions.

This design is often ideal for reference data. Reference data or parameters are often nonvolatile and updated only occasionally from one source. One can therefore make a vertical partition of the reference data, since its maintenance does not involve the other database relations.

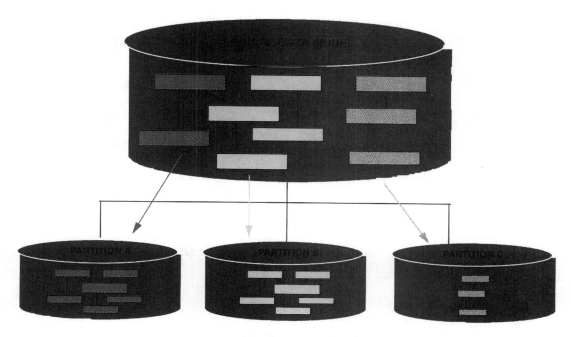

Figure 5.8 Vertical database partitioning design. The database is partitioned vertically by related entity types.

The following key issues need to be considered:

i. How many vertical segments should there be and what would be the typical size of a grouping?

ii. How will transactions that are identifier intensive (and thereby horizontal) be handled?

iii. What would be needed to either resize partitions (load balancing) or add new entity types once the database is in production? The ability to resize is necessary to scale the partitions as the volume of records grows (i.e., the way to deal with growth in database size or transaction volumes is to create more partitions that can be independently updated). The ability to add new entity types is necessary to be able to evolve the database as business diversity adds demands.

The final issue with a vertical partition is its physical placement. This is a function of analyzing the locality of reference and frequency of update from step 2.

c. *Hybrid Partitioning* (Figure 5.9)

Database records (relations) are segmented and collocated by a mixture of vertical and horizontal partitioning. Some partitions are done vertically, some are done horizontally, and some are a mixture of both. The same issues as in the other cases have to be settled (i.e., how will identifier-based transactions be serviced, how will subject entity transactions be serviced, how can the database be evolved, and where should each partition be placed).

A few final points about these design alternatives:

1. As the granularity of partitioning can be one, there is an almost limitless set of possible designs.

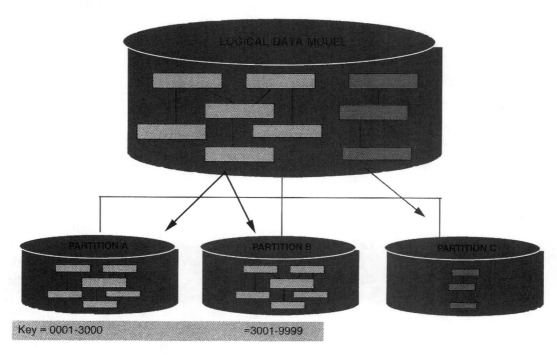

Figure 5.9   **Hybrid database partitioning. The database is partitioned with a mixture of vertical and horizontal partitioning.**

2. Sweeping elimination of alternatives is accomplished by understanding the frequency of transactions, their locality of reference, and the geography of the updaters and users. Early efforts should focus on working the problem down to a workable number of alternative scenarios.
3. All the design scenarios must maintain ACIDity though the two-phase commit protocol.
4. A single database solution is included in the set of possible solutions.
5. The partitioning design must carefully be influenced by the potential impact of distributed joins. Designs need to minimize the volume of joins that will take place across the network.

4. Database Replication (Figure 5.10)

Database replication is the creation of copies of information objects (data elements, tables, etc.) to increase performance, increase reliability, reduce cost, or deliver added functionality. Performance is increased by local reads, elimination of distributed joins, and local updates. Reliability is improved by the ability of the system to continue operating even if a primary partition is unavailable. Without replication, any database partition failure will cause the system to halt. Replication can add fault tolerance to the design. Cost savings can be incurred by trading additional storage and copying costs for reduced network traffic. Added functionality is provided by automating the delivery of data to a decision support set of databases from an OLTP set of databases.

The most obvious use for replication is to use replication facilities to automatically maintain decision support databases from the OLTP databases. There are two styles of replication:

a. *Synchronous Replication:* The replicated copy is maintained in a state of coherence with the master copy. The synchronized copy therefore must participate in the two-phase commit protocol. This type of replication is necessary to support OLTP and OSS applications where up-to-the-minute versions of data are required.
b. *Asynchronous Replication:* The replicated copy is updated at some time after the master copy. For a period of time, the replicated copy will be in a state of incoherence with the master.

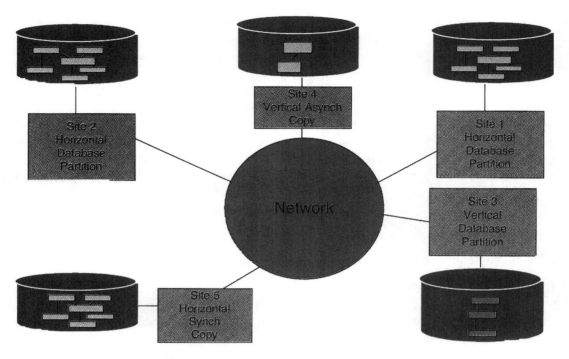

Figure 5.10   **Replication. Replication databases may be synchronous or asynchronous; they may be the same or different partitions as the original database.**

Copying may be triggered by transaction counts, by change counts, by scheduled times, manually, or by other database manger features. Asynchronous replication is suitable for moving data from the OSS/OLTP environment to the decision support environment and, in some cases, may be acceptable within an OLTP environment (looking at possibly old data is acceptable). If the OLTP environment can support some people looking at temporarily incoherent data, then the overhead of the two-phase commits can be reduced, which is the primary motivation to do asynchronous copying in the OLTP milieu.

The first issue with adding replication, then, is to decide the suitability for synchronous or asynchronous copies. The design of copies, synchronous or asynchronous, creates the need to repeat, at the copy level, the design of logical vertical copies, horizontal copies, or hybrid copies. Copies may make use of the same partitioning choices as the primary database, but it should be remembered that the partitioning scheme used can be completely different from the primary database. It should also be noted that there may be multiple copies of some information objects and no copies of other information objects. The design choices are truly inexhaustible, and, again, one must quickly use an understanding of the transactions, users, geography, and database managers to minimize the candidate scenarios.

Replication adds an additional set of flexibility choices for the distributed database designer. The main decision points are these:

1. Where will the use of synchronous and asynchronous replication improve performance, improve reliability, reduce cost, or add desired feature(s)/functionality?
2. What combinations of vertical, horizontal, and hybrid copies are required and where should they be placed (again, copies may be partitioned differently and may be incomplete)?
3. For asynchronous copies, what methods should be used to trigger the copy and how often must the copy be made?

5. Global Transparency Schema Design (Figure 5.11)

For each geographical set of users, a global transparency schema must be designed to define the view of the global logical database that they will see and update.

6. Application Program Interface (API) Design (Figure 5.12)

The distributed database is only of value if it can be accessed. It is necessary to specify the set of interfaces that will be made available to application programs to access the database. Interfaces generally fall into three groups:

1. Data manipulation languages such as SQL or embedded SQL.
2. Middleware such as SQL-ACCESS, OBDC, IADAPI, and EDA-SQL.
3. Application servers such as an e-mail message interpreter or an EDI-message interpreter.

Based on this set of interfaces both internally developed application programs and vendor software can be developed/purchased to access the distributed database.

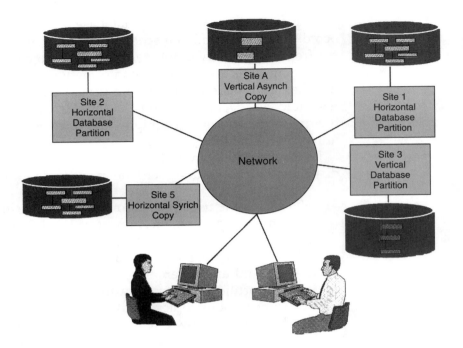

Figure 5.11   Global schema design. For each set of users, from each site, define a global transparency schema that defines a global view of the distributed database.

7. Physical Database Manager Assignments (Figure 5.13)

Actual physical database mangers are assigned to each logical database. Further decisions can now be made from two perspectives:

1. Which database managers should be used to manage which databases?
2. Which designs would appear to be implementable?

This step will most likely cause some iteration to choose new designs or modify existing designs to comply with physical database manger constraints. It is worth repeating that the issues of homogenous versus heterogeneous database managers and the same data model versus different data models resolve themselves

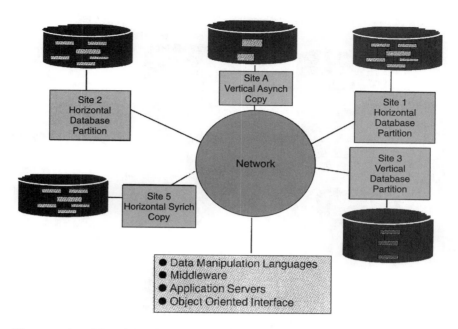

Figure 5.12   User interface design. Define the set of interfaces that will be made available to access the database

at this point. The essential question is, for a mapping of database managers to my distributed design, regardless of the homogeneity of the vendor or the data model, can I do the desired functionality?

At the end of this step, a triage has been successfully performed and one is left with a finite set of distributed database scenarios with associated database managers. It is worth noting that the same design may exist with a different combination of mangers or different managers may be used to support variant designs.

This section has presented the basic steps in designing a distributed database. A logical database must first be partitioned into a combination of vertical, horizontal, and hybrid partitions. These partitions must maintain the notion of ACIDity to maintain integrity. Replication, synchronous or asynchronous, can then be added to further the design by the dimensions of performance, availability, cost, or features/functionality.

Actual database mangers are finally assigned to the surviving designs. Figure 5.14 summarizes the design sequence. The process is

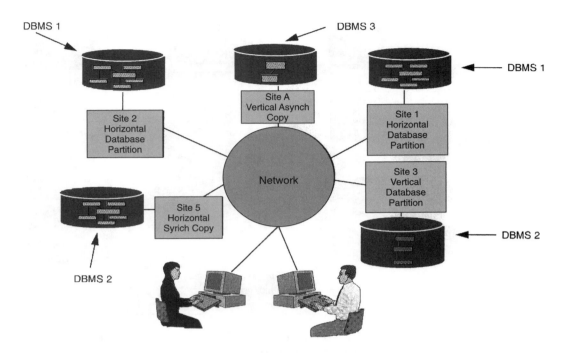

Figure 5.13   Database manager assignment. Assign a database manager to each partition and copy.

a combination of both engineering and art. The surviving scenario designs must now continue through the remaining design steps.

INDIVIDUAL DATABASE DESIGN

Each of the databases from the distributed database design is a physical database that has to be individually designed for optimum performance. Each database is designed using the following seven-step iterative process:

1. Business Analysis

The business analysis data, process, and transaction information appropriate to this partition is culled from the overall analysis that was done in support of the previous business analysis step.

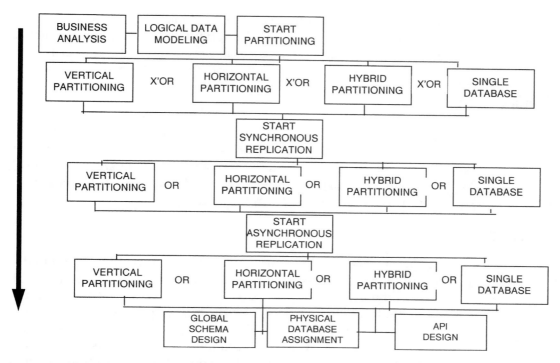

Figure 5.14 Distributed database design, consisting of eight steps.

2. Logical Data Model

A perfectly normalized logical data model of the database is developed.

3. Physical Database Design

Based on an understanding of the transaction volumes, their frequency, their priorities, their access paths, and the alternative physical design structures offered by the database manger (sequential, indexed, direct/hash, inverted list, secondary indexes, linked list, clustering, etc.), a physical design is developed.

Of particular importance is the design of the database to expeditiously support transactions that will be involved with two-phase commits and distributed joins. For OLTP and OSS databases, to assure performance, it is common to restrict the number of probable

I/Os that a transaction may incur. This may require the redesign of transactions or the databases. Important information objects such as the local schema, global schema, views, referential integrity constraints, and the rules for replication are also defined.

4. Sizing

The database is sized. This includes not only the storage requirements for the tables but the additional storage overhead requirements for indexes, pointers, and any other database overhead. Physical block sizes are often assigned in this step. Adequate space also has to be added to permit growth.

5. Space Plan

A plan is developed to map the database records to files and to distribute the files across channels and the disk subsystems. Depending on the options of the space allocation system, it is sometimes possible to explicitly place files on certain parts of disks to minimize seek time and rotational delays. Spreading the database over channels is necessary to avoid channel I/O waits. This step also has to take into account the impact of competing applications for files on the same channels and disk subsystems.[2]

6. Database Generation Options

The database manager may have options that can be "gened" to meet the specific needs of this database. Typical generation options include size of buffers, sharing of buffers, making certain tables permanently buffer resident, the number of locks, time-out parameters, and statistics gathering. If the database manager manages multiple physical databases from a single generation, this step has to balance the needs of the other databases.

7. Operating System Generation Options

Based on the database design and database generation, it may be necessary to alter operating system generation parameters. Typical parameters altered would include the definitions of interprocess communication (IPC) variables such as shared memory, semaphores, and message queues.

This process is highly iterative and will result in a set of physical databases with associated space plans, database generation plans, and operating system generation plans for each scenario. Those scenarios whose physical designs are too constrained due to database manager constraints, whose size would be prohibitive for the target platform, or whose database or operating system generation options would be inappropriate must be removed from further consideration.

BATCH PROCESSING

While it is customary to focus initial design attention on the on-line transactions to ensure adequate response time to waiting users, the reality is that batch processing, update, and reporting often is the larger, though invisible, percentage of the total workload. Optimization for batch processing often requires different design and recovery mechanisms because:

- Batch processing normally involves large units of work. (i.e., transactions update large number of records at a time and maintain locks for extended periods of time).
- There is concentrated volume. The performance issue is throughput, not response time.
- There is a need for checkpoint restart points in case of a failure, to preempt the need to restore the database and rerun the entire batch from the beginning.

To react to these demands, it is often common to sort the input to optimize passage though the database and optimize the database design to handle the batches. Optimization often includes turning database manager features on or off for only the batch run.

There are three basic design approaches to batch processing:

1. *Batch as OLTP:* The batch program presents to the system as just another transaction processing program. It mimics an interactive user. This has the benefit of permitting the exact same software to process batch and on-line transactions. The negatives are that there is no optimization for batch processing and, unless the batch programs are resident on the same processors as the databases they are accessing, network traffic may be prohibitive.

2. *Extract/Process/Update:* An extract is taken of the relevant records from the database and then in traditional batch sequential processing mode, the batch updates are processed against the extract file. The resultant file is then reapplied to the database. For this to work, there must be a rapid bulk extract and load capability and there must be a window during which the on-line system is down.

3. *Batch/Data Collocation:* The batch programs run as traditional long-running batch transactions against the database but run on the same processor as the database. This eliminates network traffic (assuming transactions only process collocated database partitions) and also permits parallelism, as separate batch jobs can run against each distributed database segment. This requires elaborate restart procedures and will often negatively effect on-line transaction processing response time if the on-line system must remain up.

The following key issues must be analyzed:

- Does it make sense to run batch with all replicated copies off-line and propagate replication after? This would include synchronized replicated copies. Would it be faster to run batch replication against the master copy only and propagate and eliminate simultaneous updates, or is it better to permit all replication to occur per design?
- Can the input be sorted to match the database partitions and thereby permit parallel batch streams to independently update different partitions of the database?
- Should batches run as a single threaded job with locking, deadlock, and so on disabled? Would it be faster to run the batches as a single linear thread without integrity overhead? This demands that the on-line systems be down during the batch run and that replication propagation occur after conclusion of the run.
- Do the batch runs disqualify certain scenario designs, or do designs have to be modified?

Normally, there is a batch off-time window during which it is highly desirable or absolutely necessary to complete all batch runs. This design step must alter the scenario distributed databases to assure this capability.

INITIAL LOADING OF THE DISTRIBUTED DATABASE

The initial batch loading of the database, though it only occurs once, has to be carefully prepared for. In addition to all the normal batch issues, the initial load is more problematic because of

1. The concentrated volume within a finite conversion time window.
2. The real possibility of the need for reruns or restarts.
3. The added transaction overhead due to the mass building of indexes and other physical data structures (in some cases, on initial loads, indexes are not built and are built in a separate step to expedite the load).

The scenario distributed databases need to be analyzed to propose how the initial load(s) will be executed against them.

TRANSACTION MONITORS

In the legacy mainframe environment, it was customary to have a transaction monitor between the transaction processing programs and the database. The transaction monitor provided many features including the ability to load balance, vary transactions on-line and off-line, and segregate transactions into performance queues. In this way priorities could be tuned and expensive transactions (in terms of CPU or I/O) could be throttled.

The design issue in a distributed database environment is whether a distributed transaction monitor should be inserted into the design. Without a transaction monitor, each requester will directly link to the database (Figure 5.15). With a transaction monitor (Figure 5.16), there are two alternatives:

1. The transaction monitor picks up the SQL and delivers it to the database server.
2. Requesters send named messages with data variables to an application data server, which then issues the SQL. This essentially creates an objectlike interface between the application requesters and the database and further decouples the processing layer from the data layer.

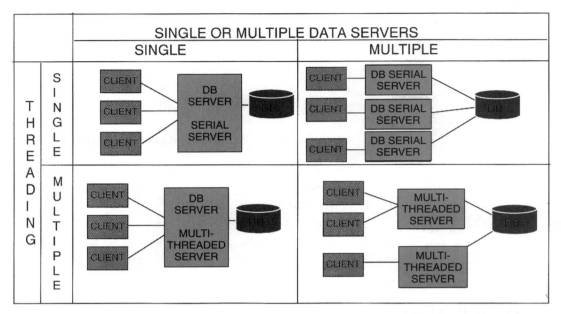

Figure 5.15   Database server designs. Database server design is a function of how many servers can coexist and whether each server is single or multithreaded.

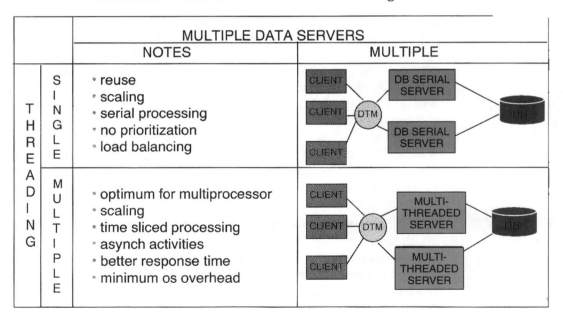

Figure 5.16   Distributed transaction monitors. By introducing a distributed transaction monitor, resources are more efficiently used by the database servers.

In either case, the transaction monitor features would provide an additional set of capabilities to improve run-time performance by load balancing, queuing, transaction priority setting, transaction throttling, and server reuse.

The key design questions are these:

- Should we insert a transaction monitor into the scenario designs?
- What does inserting a transaction monitor do to the designs?
- Will the database managers work with the desired transaction monitors?
- Does the insertion of a transaction monitor make discarded designs viable?
- Can batch programs use the transaction monitor and does it alter the batch design?

The result of this activity is a further refined set of distributed database design scenarios.

It should be mentioned that the utilization of a transaction monitor or not is often a global architecture decision of the installation and is resolved not on a case-by-case basis but based on the overall client/server architecture.

LIFE-CYCLE DISTRIBUTED DATABASE MAINTENANCE

The strategic rationale for distributed databases, as we presented in Chapter 2, is not solely to save money, improve reliability, or improve performance but to position the I/T data assets so that they can endlessly reconfigure themselves in harmony with the constantly shifting business environment diversity. It is therefore a critical design issue to understand the mechanics of changing the design once it has gone into production.

If we assume, for each remaining distributed database scenario, that the system is up and running, it is desirable to evaluate the impact of life-cycle database maintenance on the design. Is the design easy to evolve with changing times and circumstances, or having built this design, are we stuck with it and have contradicted our own intent? There are basically five actions that can be taken against the scenario database designs and their internal objects:

1. We may wish to *add* new objects (e.g., data elements, tables, partitions, replicated databases, etc.).
2. We may wish to *modify* existing information objects (e.g., change the size of a data element or the data type of a data element).
3. We may wish to *delete* information objects (.e.g., remove a data element or a table).
4. We may wish to *resize* objects (e.g., resize a partition).
5. We may wish to *move* objects (e.g., change the physical location of a replication database).

In performing these functions, we must answer these questions:

1. With what combination of manual and automated tools is the action accomplished?
2. Are the changes, as appropriate, automatically propagated throughout the distributed databases or do we have to maintain coherence ourselves?
3. Must the system be down to make the changes or can they be made with the system up and running?
4. When is unloading and reloading necessitated to perform the changes?
5. Are directories and schemas automatically maintained throughout the distributed database environment to reflect changes?
6. Can the person doing the change be remote or does she have to be local to the database?
7. If changes are not automatically propagated, can the system still run with partial changes in place or do all associated impacted objects have to be simultaneously altered?
8. Are audit trails provided to provide a permanent record of all changes?

At this point, there are *n* surviving scenario distributed database designs. While it is obviously crucial that the initial design work, it is equally critical that the design can be altered rapidly and with coherence to evolve to the changing environment. Those scenarios that demonstrate themselves to be "frozen solid" designs are undesirable and should be removed from further consideration,

OPERATIONS, ADMINISTRATION, AND DESIGN (OA&M)

The implemented distributed database system is a sophisticated and complicated engineered product that has to be designed to be production operable. Service guarantees to users are often provided in the terms of performance measures, availability measures, and time to administer. Guarantees cannot be given or realized without a realistic operations service plan.

For each surviving scenario, a plan must be proposed consisting of interwoven software products and manual procedures to perform the following tasks:

1. Software Release Management
   How will the database software be distributed, licenses administrated, installed, tested, and backed out under a formal change control mechanism? How will the installations be multisite coordinated?

2. Performance Management
   How will trend analysis, tuning, bottleneck resolution, preventive tuning, and so on be performed?

3. Backup/Restore
   How will full and incremental backups be taken? How will distributed backups be coordinated and archiving be performed?

4. Database Administration
   How will the databases be brought up and down? How will space be managed? What tools will be available to check indexes, pointers, or other database structures? As the database grows, how will resizing and additional space planning be accomplished? How will recovery journals be off-loaded, coordinated, and archived? How will logs be off-loaded, reviewed, analyzed, and archived?

5. Security Administration
   How will permissions for database access be administered? How will the database files be secured? How will incidents be traced and investigated?

6. Fault Management
   Who will users call with problems and what tools will be available to assist the help desk person? How will problem escalation work? What procedures will be in place to provide vendor support? How will troubles be identified and tracked, problems isolated and resolved?

7. Job Management
   How will batch jobs be submitted, scheduled, and monitored, and how will output (paper, microfilm, tapes, CD-ROM, etc.) be distributed?

8. Foreign Media Management
   How will foreign input tapes be managed, and how will output media be dispersed?
9. Configuration Management
   How will the documentation of the distributed database architecture be maintained? What configuration management procedures will be followed to amend the configuration?
10. Accounting
    How will users be charged back for database utilization?
11. Disaster Recovery
    How will service be restored following various disaster scenarios (i.e., loss of a database partition, loss of a processor, loss of networking, loss of a facility, etc.).

The plans for the surviving scenarios need to be compared, and those that are too costly, too labor intensive, too time-consuming, and so on should result in the corresponding scenarios being eliminated.

OA&M design culminates with the design of a Customer Satisfaction Measurement System (CSMS) that will be used to operationally measure service. Figure 5.17 illustrates a sample measurement system. An OA&M design that cannot meet established service thresholds is a prima facie criterion to eliminate the corresponding distributed database scenario from further consideration.

MODELING

The design of a distributed database environment is best described as a systems engineering task, and, as is customary with such endeavors, multiple types of modeling are required. Four types of modeling are needed:

1. *Feasibility Modeling:* The purpose of this modeling activity is to ascertain the actual capabilities of each candidate database manager to support distributed database functionality such as partitioning, replication, and two-phase commit. This modeling would be done prior to and during database partitioning and replication design to provide guidance as to what features are actually available on each candidate database manager. This modeling is limited to capability validation and is not concerned with stress testing or volume testing.

Customer View of Distributed Database Services		I/T View of Distributed Database Services	
Customer Satisfier	Satisfier Driver	I/T Owning Process	Correlated Measures
Quality	Availability	Fault Management	1. outages/month 2. MTTR 3. MTBF 4. total time unavailable/month 5. percent of time system brought up on time/month
	Performance	Service Delivery	1. response time 2. percent of batch completed on time/month 3. percent of input/output delivered on-time/month
Service	Speed	Security Administration	1. percent security change processed on-time 2. percent rework security change requests.

Figure 5.17 Customer service measurement system. To assure user satisfaction, the operations plan should be summarized as a set of measurements to align customer satisfiers and operation process measures.

2. *Prototype Modeling:* The purpose of this modeling activity is to ascertain that specific candidate designs work. This modeling would start during the database partitioning design and replication step and continue as the additional steps are executed that alter the designs. This modeling is limited to functionality verification.

3. *Simulation Modeling:* The purpose of this modeling activity is to predict various and crucial metrics of the remaining candidate designs. This modeling would be done once the candidate set is reduced to two or three surviving designs. This modeling is done using queuing models and other simulation techniques to predict the following types of metrics about each candidate design for both normal workloads and peak usage; interactive response times, batch throughput, availability, mean time to repair and mean time between failures, 5-year cost per transaction, time to perform initial load, time to take full backup, time to do full restore, and time to apply journal logs of size n. It is also advisable to ascertain CPU and network utilization under these conditions to ascertain a hardware and network growth chart for the environment, which is necessary to predict the 5-

year cost per transaction. Unless volume modeling is performed, simulation provides the factual basis for choosing among finalist designs.

4. *Volume Modeling:* The purpose of this modeling activity is to stress test the finalist designs under transaction and batch volumes that mimic the actual system. This modeling would be done as the final means to select a design. If you cannot find a reference account that is doing a similar design under similar volume and stress conditions, it is advisable to perform a stress test model to assure yourself that the database algorithms and protocols do not collapse under your unique design.

Of these four types of modeling, only the last one, volume modeling, is particularly time-consuming, labor intensive, and potentially expensive. If you cannot find a similarly designed solution under similar stress conditions, it is nevertheless advisable to do the modeling as part of the design process rather than as part of the implementation process, when the cost of reworking and the embarrassment to the development team will be exponentially higher.

RISK ASSESSMENT

Throughout the entire design process, an active risk assessment activity should be executed in parallel with the other steps. Risk is the measure of the probability and severity of adverse effects. Risk assessment is the evaluation of the evolving candidate designs against three questions:

1. What can go wrong (type of failure)?
2. What is the likelihood that it will go wrong (probability of failure)?
3. What are the consequences of it going wrong (economic cost of failure)?

Risk assessment for distributed databases covers the following potential sources of failure: hardware failures, software failures, communications/networking failures, environmental failures, human failures, and organizational failures.

Threshold levels of probabilities of failure and the economic cost of failures have to be established for all types of failures and designs evaluated against them. Designs must be revised to maintain system risk within acceptable tolerances. Figure 5.18 provides a sample worksheet for performing risk analysis.

IMPLICATIONS

Collectively, the issues that have been presented have broad implications for the information technology organization. Specifically, the impact of distributed database design should be considered on the following ten topics:

1. *Standards:* Adherence to standards is critical to successful implementations. The ability to evolve the distributed database to maintain synchrony with the shifting environmental diversity will be significantly restrained if proprietary interfaces are chosen.

Classification of Failure	Specific Type of Failure	Probability of Failure	Threshold Probability of Failure	Economic Consequence of Failure	Threshold Economic of Failure
Hardware					
Software					
Communications					
Human					
Organizational					

Figure 5.18   Risk analysis. Since distributed database design is a systems engineering activity, formal risk analysis should be performed throughout the process.

2. *Data Administration:* Proper data administration is elevated in importance in the distributed database environment. If the definition of data elements is not treated as the most fundamental standard, creating a transparent view of incompatible data definitions will be extremely difficult if not impossible. Batch copy systems compensated for poor data administration by translating data definitions during the batch runs. This hiding of data administration failure will not be available to interactive users and will compromise the fundamental purpose of a distributed database.

3. *Systems Engineering:* In the traditional mainframe environment, databases were designed and tended to by database administrators. In the distributed database environment, distributed databases must be designed by distributed database system engineers and their operability support systems (OA&M) designed by distributed database operations engineers. Database design and tending evolves from designing and tending to "a" database to designing a cohesive system of databases.

4. *Organizational Structure:* Traditional I/T organizations were often designed about technology-centric vertical smokestacks. The essence of distributed database design is horizontal integration of multiple technologies. The organizational structure of the I/T organization has to be revised to support creating horizontal teams of designers to design and operate the distributed database environment.

5. *Process Gating:* Distributed database design is a systems engineering task, not an artistic entrepreneurial activity. Existing traditional design and review processes should be amended to include formal gating steps where adherence to the methodology issues is reviewed and checkpointed.

6. *Configuration Management:* As an engineering problem, distributed database design reduces to the assembly problem of parts, assemblies of parts, super assemblies of parts, super-super assemblies of parts, and so on and on. Appropriate tools have to be introduced into the design and operations environment to keep track of the configuration definitions and the potential impacts of changes to those definitions once stabilized.

7. *Design Documentation:* As an engineering problem. the interim and final designs need to be documented with a formal drawing technique.

8. *Implementation Strategy:* While the greatest benefit of distributed database design is the flexibility it provides to management to move in response to environmental diversity, as a practical matter management remains intensely concerned about costs. Costs are minimized in a distributed database environment through sharing and reuse (economies of sharing). An implementation plan should therefore focus on implementing a family of applications that can share the same data. This will permit maximum savings to accrue as quickly as possible. You should not be democratic in your implementation but focused.

9. *Core Competencies:* The I/T organization core competence of data management is extended to include distributed database design. Extensive education and training should be expected as distributed database design evolves from a craft in the mainframe arena to an engineering discipline.

10. *Supplier Relationships:* Supplier relationships must be reengineered to create horizontal vendor support teams. In the simplest case, platform, operating systems, communications, and database vendors will have to cooperate to ensure that their parts are delivered ready to integrate new releases. In the most difficult cases, heterogeneous combinations of each type of vendor will have to cooperate to deliver ready-to-integrate parts. The I/T organization will have to function less as a tester and more as a system integrator of all their components. This will not be possible if they do not coordinate releases. Additionally, problem resolution will become an impossible finger-pointing maze without joint support.

Essentially, all aspects of the I/T organization need to be analyzed to determine how they have to be repositioned, if at all, to support a distributed database.

SUMMARY

The purpose of this chapter was to provide an analysis of the issues surrounding designing and implementing distributed databases in a client/server environment. For the vast majority of the 40-year history of commercial data processing, databases have been designed and operated, for the most part, on centralized mainframes. Business motivations coupled with advances in distributed processing technologies have made it both desirable and possible to distribute data across the enterprise while maintaining data integrity and global accessibility. Distributing data requires a data architecture, a data placement strategy, and the design and operation of distributed databases, all of which require new information technology skills and design methodologies.

This chapter has structured the issues that must be addressed in providing a coherent and effective distributed data architecture for the business and has presented at a logical and pragmatic level a taxonomy of the issues that must be considered to effectively make the transition from centralized data management to distributed data management. Since the analysis is done at a logical level, it is suitable for addressing problems that include heterogeneous as well as homogeneous environments. By implementing a distributed database, you overlay data flexibility and cost efficiency on the business environmental diversity.

NOTES

1. This section is an extract from *Implementing Client/Server Computing,* Bernard H. Boar, McGraw-Hill, 1993.
2. Some storage management systems, such as RAID, usurp the ability to do a space plan, as the storage management system performs all space assignments.

6

Reengineering the Information Technology Organization for Client/Server Computing

Eventually, after the formal presentation is completed, whether during the question and answer session or the coffee break, the question of questions is asked: "How do you do it? How do you jump the abyss from the mainframe S curve to the client/server S curve while keeping everything running and avoiding disruption and chaos? How do you reengineer the I/T organization to achieve both the cost and flexibility benefits that are promised? How?" Whether they are in the process of moving, are planning to move, will never move, or just can't make up their minds about moving, they all share the wish to know *how*.

It is a most appropriate, reasonable, important, and inevitable question. A strategy, however enticing, that is not executable is no strategy at all. The audience keenly realizes that they do not enjoy the luxuries of a desert start. To the contrary, they normally begin their migration from an up and running, overgrown I/T jungle. All they can see ahead is a list of endless and seemingly insurmountable obstacles:

- How will I sustain the embedded infrastructure and applications while rapidly introducing the C/S environment?
- How will I minimize the cost of the migration?
- How will I design, implement, and evolve a robust enterprise-wide I/T architecture?
- What tools shall I use and what processes shall I adopt to perform production OA&M?

179

- In what shall I retrain my staff? What new core competencies are required?
- How will I do batch processing in a C/S world?
- How will I build and sustain organizational commitment to my C/S vision?
- How will I overcome staff resistance, at all levels, to change?
- What processes will I have to add, modify, and delete?
- How do I become a systems integrator of heterogeneous technologies?
- How???

The act of answering the *how* questions transforms a deep and far-reaching vision for the I/T organization into executable strategic actions.

STRATEGIC REPOSITIONING

The fundamental approach that I suggest clients utilize to define and manage their migration strategy is called *strategic repositioning*. Strategic repositioning is a generic technique that provides an overarching framework for the design and management of the migration between S curves. While the details of each client's starting situation are unique and the desired future state reflects the particulars of each client's vision, strategic repositioning is sufficiently robust and flexible to provide a singular framework for all.

The root notions of strategic repositioning are as follows:

- The state of a business, at any time, can be expressed as a set of selected positions. Each position represents the state of a chosen business area, function, process, etc. What you choose to position is decided by the strategy team. You pick what is strategically important to your business.
- The position of the business (P_B) at time T is equal to the set of selected positions; that is, $P_B = (P_{\text{Financial Position}}, P_{\text{Market Position}}, P_{\text{Competencies Position}}, P_{\text{Processes Position}}, P_{\text{Human Resource Practices Position}}, P_{\text{Supplier Relationships Position}}, P_{\text{Internal Economy Position}}, P_{\text{Distribution Channels Position}}, P_{\text{etc.}})$
- A position may define itself as a set of positions. Position definition is a recursive concept, and this permits complicated

positions to be defined by decomposition. So we could say that $P_{=B} = (P_{\text{Financial Position}}, P_{\text{Market Position}}, P_{\text{Competencies Position}}, P_{\text{Processes Position}}, P_{\text{Human Resource Practices Position}}, P_{\text{Supplier Relationships Position}}, P_{\text{Internal Economy Position}}, P_{\text{Distribution Channels Position}}, P_{\text{etc.}})$ but $P_{\text{Market Position}} = (P_{\text{Product 1 Position}}, P_{\text{Product 2 Position}}, P_{\text{Product 3 Position}})$. The recursion can be repeated as many times as required to meaningfully and unambiguously express the business position.

- If we can accept that $P_{\text{Current Business Positions}}$ represents the state of the business today, then we can also imagine and design a desired future state for the business and define it as $P_{\text{Future Business Positions}}$.
- Repositioning then is the definition of
  - $P_{\text{Current Business Positions}}$,
  - $P_{\text{Future Business Positions}}$,
  - The necessary strategic actions (initiatives, moves, acts) to move the organization, in a holistic and coherent manner, between positions.

In this way, you define where you are, where you wish to be, a desired future state, for all areas of strategic concern, and how you will achieve the migration between them in an orderly, efficient, and effective manner.

It is not surprising that the motivation for this approach can be traced to *The Art of War*. Sun Tzu said

> The victories of good warriors are not known for cleverness or bravery. Therefore their victories are not flukes. Their victories are not flukes because they *position* themselves where they will surely win, prevailing over those who have already lost.

So our strategy must focus on defining a winning set of future positions for the I/T organization that will ensure a total victory over those who have already lost.

STRATEGIC REPOSITIONING EXAMPLES

We will now provide ten examples of this method. The examples are deliberately concise, as it is our intent to illustrate the method and not the final answer. Each migrating organization would complete the repositioning framework in a manner particular to its own starting situation, culture, constraints, aspirations/ambitions, and vision.[1] While the strategic dimensions that will be illustrated are certainly key areas, again, what areas are to be modeled and the method of modeling must be decided by each strategy team.

1. Repositioning Issue: I/T Architecture
Description: The I/T architecture defines the information technology elements that compose your I/T resources and the rules for their interaction. It defines the infrastructure that enables fluid information exchange both across the enterprise and with its value chain business partners.

Exemplary Current Position: A host-centered computing architecture that is hardware centric and primary vendor defined. The architecture equates to the vendors' key products (Figure 1.7).

Exemplary Desired Future Position: An open, standards based, and heterogeneous client/server architecture that is software centric (Figure 1.11). The architecture is horizontal in nature and is defined by the user.

Exemplary Strategic Actions:

  a. Create an architecture definition team with the mandate to define a reach, range, and maneuverable architecture for the business (Figure   3.15).
  b. Develop a process to maintain the architecture centered around an Architecture Review Board.
  c. Develop a process to perform architectural reviews of new projects.
  d. Educate the I/T and user communities about the importance of architecture and your architecture strategy.
  e. Implement a pollution tax on those projects that violate the architecture and pollute your I/T environment.

2. Repositioning Issue: Core Competencies
Description: Core competencies are the root skills from which value emanates. Well-selected and well-developed core competencies are leveraged into supporting multiple products and services.

Exemplary Current Position: Most mainframe oriented organizations are competent in the broad areas of mainframe processing, wide area data communications, and application development. This results in being able to deliver to the clients the three products of production systems operation, new application development and system maintenance. Figure 6.1 illustrates this competency structure.

Exemplary Desired Future Position: The skill base to support client/server computing requires the building of six core competencies. These competencies support the two core products of Infrastructure Products/Services Operations and Applied I/T. Figure 6.2 illustrates the client/server core competency model and the resulting seven key products and services that are delivered to the clients.

Exemplary Strategic Actions:

    a. Perform a competency audit.
    b. Develop an education and skill building plan.
    c. Develop a mentor/apprenticeship plan.

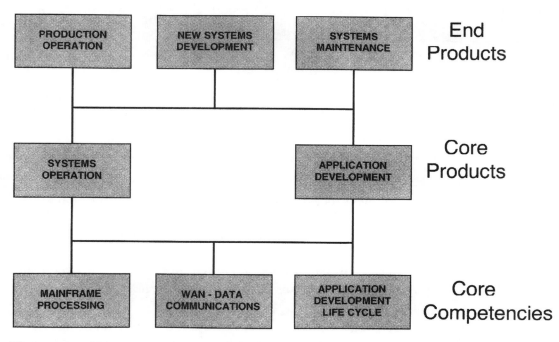

Figure 6.1   **Host-centered core competencies. To provide quality services in support of mainframe computing, the I/T organization requires three core competencies.**

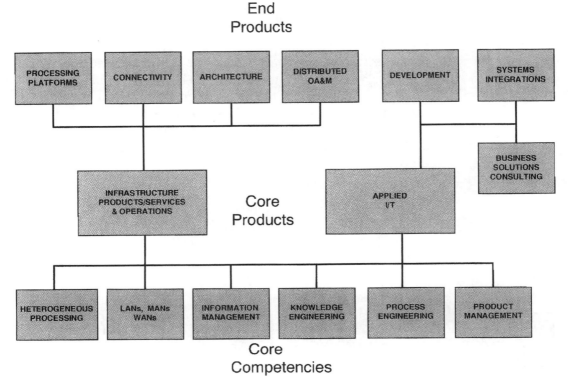

Figure 6.2   Client/server core competencies. To provide quality services in support of client/serve computing, the I/T organization requires six core competencies.

3. *Repositioning Issue:* Processes

Description: Processes are the ordered set of activities that are executed to deliver value to a customer. The I/T organization is a business just like any other business and must optimize its processes to deliver efficient and effective value.

Exemplary Current Position: As illustrated in Figure 6.3, there are only two key processes needed to support host-centered computing.

Exemplary Desired Future Position: As illustrated in Figure 6.4, client/server computing requires the implementation of six key processes.

	PROCESS SPEED	PROCESS CONSISTENCY	AGILITY	CROSS-FUNCTIONAL	BEGIN & END WITH CUSTOMER	EFFICIENT
APPLICATION DEVELOPMENT						
SYSTEMS OPERATION						

Figure 6.3   Host-centered processes. Two key processes were necessary to support host-centered computing.

	PROCESS SPEED	PROCESS CONSISTENCY	AGILITY	CROSS-FUNCTIONAL	BEGIN & END WITH CUSTOMER	EFFICIENT
APPLICATION DEVELOPMENT						
DISTRIBUTED SYSTEMS OPERATION						
SYSTEMS INTEGRATION						
PROVISIONING						
ARCHITECTURE						
SOLUTIONS CONSULTING						

Figure 6.4   Client/server processes. Six key processes are necessary to support client/server computing.

Exemplary Strategic Actions:

   a. Sponsor process reengineering teams.
   b. Benchmark to discover best processes.
   c. Infuse processes with I/T to infuse advantage.
   d. Use prototyping and pathfinder projects to discover the way.

4. *Repositioning Issue:* Human Resource Policies
Description: Human resource policies are the systems and credos that the business uses to convert business values into employee behaviors.

Exemplary Current Position: A typical mainframe organization will illustrate the following behaviors by their staff:

- *Monopolist:* Staff members believe that they own I/T and will deliver I/T services how and when they choose.
- *"A" Skill Set:* Staff members are competent in a particular technology. They see themselves as IMS/DB experts as opposed to being database experts who happen to be working on IMS/DB. Some employees have spent a career nurturing a set of skills.
- *Technology Focused:* Staff members are enamored with bits, bytes, pixels, widgets, packets, MIPS, and DRAMs. They know little about the business and, in many ways, are more an extension of the hardware vendor than their own employer.
- *Individualist:* Staff members solve their specific problems. They don't see or understand their component as part of a greater product or process.
- *Artisan:* Work is performed in an artisan mode.

These behaviors are incompatible with a client/server environment.

Exemplary Desired Future Position: A client/server organization will need to exhibit the following types of behaviors:

- *Competitor:* Staff members understand that they earn their salaries by serving a customer. They only will maintain their jobs by offering ever-improved value propositions at ever-decreasing costs.

- *Continuous Learning:* Staff members continually learn new skills and technologies. They become masters of an area (e.g., a database expert or a human interface expert) rather than masters of a particular technology.
- *Business Solution Focused:* Staff members understand that the purpose of I/T is to enable the business to build and sustain advantage. Technology has no value unto itself.
- *Team Player:* Staff members understand that client/server solutions are horizontal combinations of technology. Services cannot be delivered to clients without extensive teamwork across environments.
- *Engineer:* Client/server environments are understood to be sophisticated systems engineering problems. Staff members evolve to being system engineers from system artisans.

Exemplary Strategic Actions:

   a. Define business values.
   b. Define winning behaviors.
   c. Revise human resource systems to strongly reward winning behaviors and strongly discourage dated behaviors.

5. *Repositioning Issue:* Products and Services
Description: Products and services are what you sell to your customers.

Exemplary Current Position: Many host-centered sites offer *one size fits all* computing.

Exemplary Desired Future Position: Users require flexibility from their I/T assets. Some user organizations will be growing, some contracting, some competing in specialized markets, some competing on cost, and some competing on value added. As shown in Figure 6.5, the client/server I/T organization needs to provide a variety of related offerings.

Exemplary Strategic Actions:

   a. Implement product management system.
   b. Define products and services.
   c. Market a variety of solutions at varied value propositions to meet users' diverse needs.

6. *Repositioning Issue:* Internal Economy
Description: The internal economy defines the rules of exchange between the I/T organization and the user organizations and

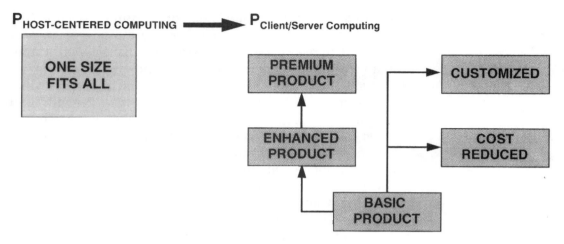

Figure 6.5   **Product/service variety. The reengineered I/T organization will offer a medley of products and services with diverse but complementary value propositions.**

the rules of exchange between entities within the I/T organization.

Exemplary Current Position: The relationship between the I/T organization and that of the user organizations is often one of an internal monopolist. The relationships between I/T organizational entities is often best characterized as warring feudal states.

Exemplary Desired Future Position: Internal market economy where I/T units are paid for services rendered by users who control their own I/T budgets.

Exemplary Strategic Actions:

    a. Initiate activity to model the current economic system that operates within the business.

    b. Design and implement a new internal economy based on the principals of an internal marketplace.

7. *Repositioning Issue:* Organization Structure
Description: The organizational structure defines the formal organizational hierarchy and reporting structure.

Exemplary Current Position: Vertical smokestacks by technology.

Exemplary Desired Future Position: Organizational objects that are cut and pasted together to deliver processes.

Exemplary Strategic Actions:

- a. Partition the I/T organization into functional objects that advertise services that they perform.
- b. Designate service owners who deliver services by cutting and pasting the object services together.

8. *Repositioning Issue:* Management Philosophy
Description: The defining attitudes that reflect the beliefs of the management team.

Exemplary Current Position: Hierarchical decision making that is fascinated with I/T fads.

Exemplary Desired Future Position: Sunian strategists who develop deep and far-reaching strategies and empower their employees to implement them.

Exemplary Strategic Actions:

- a. All members of the management team to undergo training in the teachings of *The Art of War.*
- b. Management decisions are evaluated and debated based on *The Art of War*'s teachings.
- c. Annual recertification of management staff on *The Art of War* acumen.

9. Repositioning Issue: Planning
Description: The planning system used by the I/T organization.

Exemplary Current Position: Focused almost exclusively on technology planning.

Exemplary Desired Future Position: I/T organization treated as a logical strategic business unit. Strategic business planning implemented that includes technology planning but addresses all business issues as required (Figure 6.6).

Exemplary Strategic Actions:

- a. Select and implement a strategic business planning methodology.

10. *Repositioning Issue:* Supplier Relationships
Description: The policies and attitudes that govern dealing with suppliers.

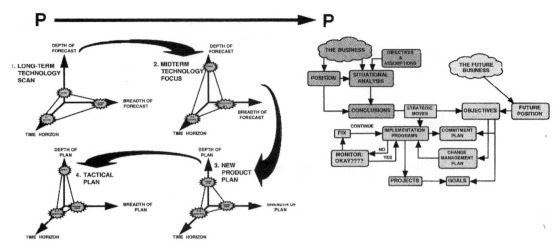

Figure 6.6   Planning reengineering. The new I/T organization must do strategic business planning that includes traditional technology planning.

Exemplary Current Position: Adversarial.

Exemplary Desired Future Position: Strategic business partner with horizontal vendor support teams.

Exemplary Strategic Actions:

   a. Define a policy statement on how you insist that vendors with whom you do business behave.
   b. Implement a new vendor relationships system.

Figure 6.7 summarizes the reengineering endeavor. In designing all the future positions, as well as any others we may choose, we must not repeat the errors of the past. What we should have learned is that the business environment continues to get ever more turbulent. We therefore must design future positions that are infused with flexibility, agility, dexterity, adaptability, and nimbleness. These attributes are not something that is appended to the positions; they must be in the inherent character of the positions. Winning positions are positions that permit the business to maneu-

REENGINEERING I/T IS MOVEMENT FROM:

$P_{HOST\ CENTERED}$ ⟶ $P_{Client/Server}$

• **Architecture**	• **Architecture**
• **Core competencies**	• **Core competencies**
• **Capabilities (processes)**	• **Capabilities (processes)**
• **Human resources**	• **Human resources**
• **Products/services**	• **Products/services**
• **Economy**	• **Economy**
• **Supplier relationships**	• **Supplier relationships**
• **Planning**	• **Planning**
• **Management philosophy**	• **Management philosophy**
• **Organization structure**	• **Organization structure**

Figure 6.7   Reengineering summary. Reengineering the I/T organization means moving it from a set of current defining positions to a new and winning set of positions.

ver. They must be designed to support a business that is formless
like water and adapts its shape continually to ever-changing times
and circumstances rather than a business that is like a glacial block
of immobile ice.

It should be obvious that we are not suggesting that you merely
reengineer a process. We are providing a framework to reinvent an
organization in its entirety. This is required because your organization, however well designed and run, was designed to support
mainframe computing. You must holistically reengineer yourself
because client/server computing is a radically different animal and
makes obsolete many, if not all, of your mainframe practices. If you
only address selected pieces of your organization, the new pieces
will be in constant friction with the antiquated pieces and the result
will be incredible and unproductive battling. Your staff will
exhaust themselves with internal brawling rather than delivering
value to your customers. You must comprehend the scope of the
effort that your undertake and prepare yourself and your plan
appropriately.

CHANGE MANAGEMENT AND COMMITMENT

While it is to be expected that I/T people would focus their attention and energy on technology issues, the reality is that the most difficult part of the reengineering process is not technology issues but people issues. Technology is inanimate; it doesn't push back. It either works or it doesn't, and if it doesn't, with time, money, and effort, you make it work. Problems that are solvable by just spending money are actually the simplest kinds of problems to solve. People, on the other hand, have all kinds of vested interests in what is and they push back to protect and maintain their inviolate rights in the status quo. So if one studies the history of change, one learns that those who were most successful were those who focused a generous portion of their time, planning, and energy on the people issues of change management and commitment.

Each of these is a huge subject and it is our intent in this section only to raise the issues so that the definition of strategic repositioning is complete. Once you have modeled where you are, where you wish to be, and the mechanics of how you will leap the chasm, you must plan and foresee how you will deal with benign and active resistance to change (change management) and how you will maintain extended organizational effort to the endeavor (commitment management).

Nothing is as hard to overcome as the opposing will of people. Many will have social, educational, status, power, political, control, prestige, or other reasons to wish to maintain the current set of positions. Your impeccably reasoned and correct arguments will fall on deaf ears. Even if they are not thriving in the current situation, they know the rules of the game, and change provides not opportunity but anxiety and risk. So overtly or covertly, many will resist. Since nothing can be accomplished without the efforts of the staff, it is virgin innocence to believe that they will instantly and voluntarily accept *big* change. Anticipating resistance and developing a plan to overcome it is not only shrewd planning, it is mandatory planning.

Creating and sustaining commitment is complementary to change management. Many employees are quite jaded and cynical of all management initiatives. They believe that each new major change project is simply today's fad and, if they wait a few days, *this too will pass.* Commitment is a problem at all levels. Executives have notoriously fleeting attention spans, middle management adeptly balances the strategy against their own well-being, and the organizational proletariat is tired of being blown over by the continually changing directions. But commitment remains vital to success. Commitment brings belief, and belief yields extended and Herculean effort. Herculean effort is what is needed to bridge the abyss between S curves, but Herculean effort is only a derivative of commitment. So you must develop a plan of how you will first demonstrate and then sustain commitment throughout the migration process. No commitment assures no success. You must develop a plan that proves, to even the most skeptical, that this time, you mean it.

As shown in Figure 6.8, as I/T architecture has evolved, the level of complaining has correspondingly escalated. This reaction of complaint rather than opportunity is what must be dealt with by your change and commitment plans. To keep this in perspective and not be overwhelmed by the challenge of change, it is good to remember the accomplishments of change masters like Mustafa Kemal Ataturk. Ataturk is the father of modern Turkey and lead a massive social transformation in Turkey in the 1920s that included:

- Redefining people's identify from citizens of the Ottoman Empire to citizens of a Turkish nation.
- Changing the basis of the state from a theocracy to a secular state.

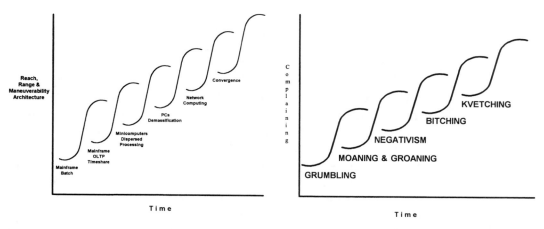

Figure 6.8   Architecture and complaint "S" curves. As architecture has evolved the level of complaining has correspondingly escalated.

- Changing dress customs from religious to lay dress.
- Changing the alphabet from the Arabic alphabet to the Latin alphabet.
- Changing the legal system from Muslim law to the Swiss legal system.
- Escalating women to a state of legal gender equality in society.

Ataturk changed the economic, social, legal, cultural and religious structure of his country. As hard as moving to client/server computing is, people have overcome much greater challenges.

When I am discouraged in a situation of change, I recall the inspiring words of General George Marshall, Chief of Staff, U.S. Army in World War II, who wrote to his commanders:

> Campaigns and battles are nothing but a series of difficulties to be overcome The lack of equipment, the lack of food or this or that is only excuses. The real leader displays his quality in his triumph over adversity however great it may be.

There is no easy rite of passage across "S" curves. There is no magician you can hire to say some mumbo jumbo over your project and make it easy. The secret to the endless trials of change is summed up in one word: *overcome*.

SUMMARY

This chapter has provided a generic approach to developing a strategy to reengineer the I/T organization to support client/server computing. The approach views the problem as one of reinventing the I/T organization. You must not merely reengineer a process, you must redesign your organization in toto. An I/T organization can be modeled as a set of positions. These positions define the composite state of the I/T organization. Client/server represents *big* change. Most, if not all, of the positions of the I/T organization, regardless of excellence, reflect an organization that was designed to support host-centered computing. Client/server represents a radically different technology, and it is therefore necessary to design new positions that realign the I/T organization. Special care must be taken to address the people issues of change management and commitment management. In this way, your thinking on how your enterprise will migrate to client/server will be "deep and far-reaching." Consequently, your plan will position you so that you will already have won even before you execute it.

NOTES

1. More specifics on positioning in general and more detailed and specific future positions are presented in my other books.

7

The Art of War and Client/Server Computing

The finest book ever written on strategy is *The Art of War*. Written over 2500 years ago by a philosopher/warrior, Sun Tzu, the book has remained a peerless and perennial store of strategic value, insight, and wisdom. It has remained perpetually relevant, has transcended radically changing times and circumstances, and provides ever-emergent and refreshing ways to cope with strategic conflict. As is common with all works of genius, it rations its wisdom in proportion to the reader's readiness and preparation to receive. The challenge in being a student of *The Art of War* is to be worthy to understand and appreciate the depth of its messages. Although explicitly a book on military strategy, it is really a general treatise on conflict and could just as well have been titled "The Art of Strategic Conflict." The subject of the book is all the strategic dimensions of conflict including the psychological, the social, and the physical. It is a grand challenge to attempt to reduce *The Art of War* to a set of strategic themes. The messages of the book are presented through aphorisms, and much is lost when summarizing the ideas into an innate and cold tabular list. Nevertheless, with apologies, according to Sun Tzu, this, and only this, is what matters:[1]

- *Assessment:* It is the responsibility of the leadership to fully assess the situation before committing its forces to conflict. Based on the assessment, an overarching strategy is adopted. Tactical maneuver and adaptation take place within this strategy.
- *Alliances:* It is the responsibility of the leadership to develop a community of allies. The strength of the alliance is stronger than the simple additive strength of the individual members.

- *Structure:* Structure depends on strategy. Forces are to be structured so as to enable the realization of the strategy.
- *Indirection:* Opponents should not be confronted directly. The maximum gain at the minimum expense is achieved by deception, surprise, and chipping away at the edges of the opponent. Exhaust them before you confront them.
- *Speed:* All matters require speed. Speed alone can compensate for numerous other shortcomings.
- *Strategic Conflict:* The opponent is to be contested strategically. Attack and ruin their strategy; do not engage their armies.
- *Self-Invincibility:* The first order of business is to make oneself invincible. Before engaging in expansionist activities, be sure that you cannot be defeated at home.
- *Prescience:* The leadership must have deep and far-reaching foresight. Leaders must see and know what others do not. The height of prescience is to see the formless and act on it.
- *Formlessness:* The architecture of your advantages must be inscrutable. In this way, your opponents do not know against what to attack and against what to defend.
- *Positioning:* Forces must be preplaced in winning positions by design. In this way, the actual confrontation is anticlimactic, as you have already won by your superior position.
- *Commitment:* All must share the same commitment to the objectives. Forces that do not share the same aims will lack the will and resolve to overcome the endless barriers to victory.
- *Maneuver:* Maneuver means finding the best way to go. Forces must be able to maneuver to attack at the gaps.
- *Leadership:* The leadership is responsible for the well-being of the community. Leaders must lay deep plans for what others do not foresee.
- *Efficiency:* Extended confrontations drain the community of its wealth. The best victories are swift and at the absolute minimum cost.
- *Coordination:* The problem of coordination is the problem of managing the many as though they were one. The few can defeat the many if they act with one purpose. When perfect coordination is achieved, one cannot distinguish the will of the individual from the will of the many nor the will of the many from the will of the individual.
- *Discipline:* There must be an impartial system of reward and punishment. Good leadership rewards the worthy.

- *Psychological Conflict:* Victory and defeat first occur in the mind. Defeat your opponents psychologically so that even if they are intact, they lack the will to contest you.
- *Foreknowledge:* All matters require competitive intelligence. Nothing is more important then understanding the plans of your opponents.
- *Love of the People:* True leadership is not a function of title but a function of the love of the people. Leaders must share the struggle of their forces. One must win the affection of one's troops so that they would gladly die for you.

All these themes converge on one grand theme—advantage. The struggle of conflict is the struggle for building and sustaining advantage. The one with more advantages wins; the one with fewer advantages loses. It really is that simple, yet so complex.

It would seem obvious that a technology would be of extreme interest to any manager if it could assist them in achieving even one Sunian strategic theme. How much more exciting a technology that can provide assistance in achieving nine strategic themes. Client/server provides direct assistance in achieving the following strategic themes:

- *Alliances:* C/S makes you an attractive partner because of your superior ability to perform relationship computing.
- *Organizational Structure:* C/S enables you to alter your systems to accommodate the organizational structure you require to compete. Systems adapt to the business; the business need not adapt to I/T.
- *Indirection:* C/S enables you to quickly bring you assets to windows of opportunity. You can attack where, when, and how the business demands I/T.
- *Speed:* The attributes of C/S, portability, interoperability, and reconfigurability all contribute to enabling C/S to respond rapidly to changing business requirements.
- *Strategic Conflict:* Competing strategically requires responding quickly based on what is discovered about an opponent's strategy. C/S does this by virtue of its speed and maneuverability.
- *Formlessness:* By virtue of the decoupling of the presentation, processing, and data layers and the use of standard interfaces, C/S permits one to create inexhaustible combinations of architecture.

- *Maneuver:* This is fundamental to C/S's nature.
- *Efficiency:* C/S is efficient by virtue of economies of sharing.
- *Coordination:* C/S encourages open interoperability, which permits coordination across the value chain.

In these ways, CSC enables the business to build, sustain, and compound advantage.

CSC should be understood as the first *strategic configuration of I/T.* Sun Tzu said:

> A victorious strategy is not repeated, the configurations of response to the enemy are inexhaustible. . . . Water configures its flow in accord with the terrain; the army controls its victory in accord with the enemy. Thus, the army does not maintain any constant *strategic configuration of power;* water has no constant shape. The end of an army's form is formlessness.

It is from the strategic configuration of power that a victorious strategy emanates. Since a victorious strategy is not to be repeated,

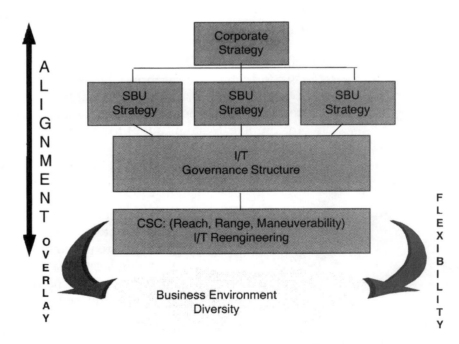

Figure 7.1   **Strategy summary. The reason to move to client/server computing is for alignment and flexibility.**

the configuration of power must be endlessly adaptable and incredibly powerful. For those who understand CSC, the creation of a strategic configuration of power for the business is the ultimate goal. For those who master CSC, the victories will be inexhaustible.

So, for those of you who approach the challenge of I/T strategy as Sunian strategists, how you assess and select technology is no mysterious art. You assess technology in terms of its ability to assist you in realizing your desired portfolio of Sunian themes. Those technologies that offer assistance are kept and cherished; those that do not are at once discarded. While it may be confusing to the MPS and the PSCS why we are moving to CSC, it is crystal clear to a Sunian strategist. The reason is advantage; the reason is the first opportunity to create a strategic configuration of I/T power that will enable the business to triumph (Figure 7.1).

EPILOGUE

The most flattering complement I have ever received in my professional life was when a colleague said to me, "Sun Tzu channels through you." This is certainly not the case. I recognize the vastly superior strategic acumen of Sun Tzu and attempt but to learn from him and do strategy as I imagine that he would. I am certainly nothing more than a novice student of the gifted master.

Nevertheless, the incident raises a most important point. As a member of the leadership of your firm, you carry a heavy responsibility to all the constituents who are depending on you: the employees, the customers, and the owners. Strategy is of primary importance to your success. If you wished to become a great composer, you would surely be a student of Mozart; if you wished to become a great sculptor, you would unquestionably be a student of Michelangelo; if you wished to be a truly great painter, you would study the magnificent works of Rembrandt; and if you wished to become a notable writer, you would study the books of Dickens. If it is your challenge to become a great strategist, you will do well to study the teachings and walk in the path of Sun Tzu.

NOTES

1. We call these ideas Sunian strategic themes.

8

The Mainframe Empire Strikes Back

I do not suspect that anyone will ever be able to accuse the I/T community of being shy or reserved in their opinions. Having presented the ideas in these chapters in Phoenix, Dallas, San Jose, San Francisco, Atlanta, Copenhagen, Amsterdam, Brussels, Oslo, Toronto, Winnipeg, Milan, London, and so on, I learned quickly that no sooner would my prepared seminar finish than the hands would shoot up. The discussions that followed were often stimulating and freewheeling, and offered a creative variety of viewpoints.

What I would like to do is share some of the questions and answers that were exchanged during those discussion periods. The format will be a statement of the question followed by my response. Obviously, the questions and answers have been altered and repackaged to fit the structure of this book and are not verbatim. As one can never anticipate all the interests and perspectives of a mixed group of readers, perhaps the questions of your peers reflect your own concerns and this section will alleviate any open issues. Since most of the questions I have selected strongly tested and probed my views, I believe that they were asked by mainframe advocates and, consequently, the title for this chapter.

Question 1:   IBM has demonstrated excellent resiliency since 1994. How can you suggest that mainframes are in trouble when the results are just the opposite? The fascination with C/S is ending as reality teaches its limits and the rebirth of our mainframes are at hand.

Answer 1:   I don't say that mainframes are in trouble, S curves do. As I argued in Chapter 3, client/server technology has launched an asset attack on mainframes. Paradoxically, during an interim period of comple-

203

mentary functionality, client/server stimulates mainframe usage. As market demand for MIPS exceeds those lost to migration and IBM's massive cost reductions kick in, IBM's results are impressive. The problem for IBM and the other mainframe PCM vendors is what happens as the attack S curve accelerates, the complementary function period erodes, and the function defense comes under assault.

The nature of the client/server S curve attack is that of a maneuver fighter. It does not attack host-centered computing at its strength. Rather, it first attacks decision support and information sharing applications in gradually increasing sizes. Next it attacks the smaller OLTP and OSS applications. Only after all these trophies have been won does it go after the final large mainframe transaction applications. As client/server chips away at the former mainframe applications, the market for mainframes keeps shrinking and reduces the customer base against which mainframe maintenance and development cost must be spread. So the client/server attack is insidious: As it picks off those applications that it does best now, it simultaneously depletes the customer base for mainframes (mainframe MIPS may be growing, but everyone agrees customers are not) and positions itself for the final attack against a weakened mainframe opponent.

In a few years, IBM will either be riding the client/server S curve or there will be no IBM. Strategic thinking must focus on what will be, not what is. It is exactly because of the result that 70% of IBM's current profits are from "Big Iron" that there is cause for concern.

Question 2: Your opinions not only are quite different (radically so) from those of mainframe supporters but also vary from mainstream C/S advocates. How do you explains the wide discrepancy? Why should we believe you?

Answer 2: The obvious answer is that I believe that my views are based on deeper and more far-reaching strategic thinking than the others. Just as there are markets for database managers, servers, routers, and all the other innumerable instruments of I/T, there is also a marketplace for ideas. We call that marketplace *thought leadership*. I compete with many able people in that marketplace and hope that by the probity of my exhaustive explanations, I will convince a meaningful market share that my ideas provide a superior path to success. Variety of opinion is healthy for the thought leadership marketplace, just as product selection is healthy in any other market. You, the consumer, decide by your purchasing decisions which ideas win and which ideas lose.

My ideas are often at odds with many others because I am more interested in being a prophet than making a profit. As a consequence, my work is strategy laden rather than I/T laden. The marketplace is clearly more interested in I/T than in strategy. If you approach the challenge of I/T strategy with the primary emphasis on strategy and the adjunct emphasis on I/T, it is not surprising that you arrive at varied conclusions; your analytical and synthesis processes are quite different. So if I balance the ratios of I/T strategy at 80% strategy and 20% I/T while many others do just the opposite, diverse viewpoints are inescapable. I believe the best way to validate my ideas, or anyone else's, is through pathfinder experiments. You do not have to proceed on faith; you can learn through calculated and control trials.

Question 3:   Aren't your arguments terribly skewed and biased? You do not present any of the shortcomings or problems with C/S. I expected a balanced presentation.

Answer 3:   It was not my intent to be a tightrope walker who delicately balances two equally valid views. If you review the citations in Appendixes A and B, you will find articles, in rich detail, that itemize the alleged shortcomings and limitations of CSC. Those citations could never be accused of being balanced. This book is an unapologetic *partisan rebuttal* that provides a meticulous refutation to the MPS and PSCS arguments. There arguments are presented elsewhere in ample quantity. If there is a market for a balanced analysis, I would anticipate that someone will hustle to close that market opportunity.

Question 4:   You didn't respond to some of the most important MPS issues (e.g., C/S integrity limitations, reliability problems, security defects, etc.). Doesn't this indicate that the MPS is right?

Answer 4:   There is a hierarchy to planning. The levels are vision, strategy, implementation programs, and projects. This is a book about vision and strategy that refutes the MPS at that level. The issues listed in your questions are very important pragmatic tactical issues. What I suggest that clients do, rather then decide these issues on gross generalizations, is to confront vendors with a list of specifics. Ask your candidate vendor to demonstrate exactly how database recovery is done, how backups are taken, how security is administered, how performance is monitored, and so on. These issues are not subject to debate; they *are* subject to demonstration.

I believe that you will be pleasantly surprised at the current and projected capabilities. Based on your assessment, you can implement C/S in a manner consistent with your view of maturity levels, level of risk aversion, and business opportunity. So the strategy is clear, it is C/S, and the tactics need to be dynamic to be in accord with constantly changing circumstances as the C/S OA&M market matures.

I believe that this questions fronts for a much more serious question: "Can you really do real computing with CSC?" Many I/T executives and their staffs have spent their entire careers essentially using one vendor's products. *Real computing* was only done on those products. It is somewhat hard to accept that what had been done, for what seemed forever, on IBM mainframes can really be done on other vendors' hardware with software from an assortment of vendors. It really can.

Question 5:   I didn't fully understand the reasoning you presented with regard to overlaying I/T flexibility upon business environmental diversity (Figure 2.17). Could you amplify?

Answer 5:   Think of a business as a set of roles performed by people. Each role has to communicate with other roles both within the company and outside the company with value chain partners. If there are n roles across the value chain, then there are $n \times (n-1)/2$ possible communication links. Any individual has $n-1$ possible communication links. If we label an active communication link as a collaboration, then we can introduce the notion of saturation where an individual's saturation equals (active personal collaborations)/$n-1$ and the business saturation level equals (all active collaborations)/$[n \times (n-1)/2]$. The saturation value is a measure of how much information exchange is occurring across the value chain.

In traditional hierarchical organizations, the saturation levels were extremely skewed. Managers would have high saturation levels, and the worker drones would have extremely low saturation levels. What is happening is that as a result of competition and the migration to the era of the knowledge worker, saturation levels are exploding and becoming much more leveled. I/T is required to enable the maximum saturation levels for both the business and the individual. In this way, information is exchanged between all roles that require information in a timely and beneficial manner. Information is the food of knowledge workers. The problem, of course, is that this information exchange must take place within the context of the environmental business diversity. So an I/T architecture must be overlaid on the diversity that will enable limitless adaptable creation and destruction of collaborations as dictated by churning business opportunities.

Question 6:   Do you have clients that have achieved the cost savings your assert through your economies of sharing model? Why didn't your provide an example of the savings?

Answer 6:   I cannot provide a reference for the costing model. The ideas presented are a theory of how to approach the costing problem. It is clear that the economies of scale model is inappropriate for costing C/S systems, so a different approach is called for. It will take time to prove the theory correct. As proof requires the purposeful development of a family of applications to achieve the kindling point, it will take time until early adopters can verify the results.

I chose not to provide a specific C/S costing example because such an example would be meaningless and easily challenged. There are so many variables that any artificial example can effortlessly be charged with being "fixed." I recommend that organizations that are adopting C/S should use the prescribed economies of sharing model, and I believe favorable results will be published within a few years.

Question 7:   Do you really expect us to junk our mainframe overnight and move to C/S based on your arguments?

Answer 7:   No, I would expect that, if you are typical, you are spending about 3% of your revenue on I/T and, of that, 50 to 70% on maintenance. Consequently, you don't have very much money to do anything overnight even if you wanted to. What I suggest is that you develop a vision for I/T and a strategy for C/S. You can then proceed with migration in an orderly and evolutionary manner. The junking of the mainframes will occur in due time without any special effort on your part.

Question 8:   Isn't this presentation exactly what the MPS asserts? You are a self-serving vendor/consultant who is simply promoting C/S for your own selfish financial gain?

Answer 8:   For a shallow and self-serving consultant, I have gone to absolutely extraordinary lengths to explain my strategic logic in agonizing and excruciating detail. I would suggest that the logic I have presented (e.g., value point, maneuver, S curves, strategic paradox, strategic vision, and economies of sharing) is far more elaborate and well reasoned then all of the MPS and PSCS logic in Appendixes A and B combined.

It is impossible to respond to an assertion that says, "If you support CSC, then you are a self-serving vendor." This is an axiom, not an argumentative question. Whatever I would say would just be further proof of my guilt. In formal logic, this type of statement, which is not subject to dispute, is called the "No True Scotsman" fallacy. The best that I can suggest is that rather than my arguing for C/S and having whatever I say be a priori denied, you provide a list of what proofs would convince you. In that way, perhaps a convincing argument could be made if the evidence required for you to change your mind were made public and could be assembled.

Question 9:   Didn't your arguments contradict each other? First you said the issue was flexibility (strategic paradox argument) and then you said that C/S was cheaper (economies of sharing argument). Which is it?

Answer 9:   C/S is both more flexible and cheaper. C/S can provide incredible adaptability and be cheaper. It is an absolutely wonderful situation. Absolutely wonderful situations occur whenever the consumer's dilemma is solved, and that is what C/S has done.

Question 10:   Do you really expect us to believe and apply this Sun Tzu strategy stuff? Isn't it absurd to base I/T strategy on the writings of a militarist who lived 2500 years ago?

Answer 10:   Absolutely and without reservation. Strategy is an intellectual discipline that must be studied and mastered with the same effort as is

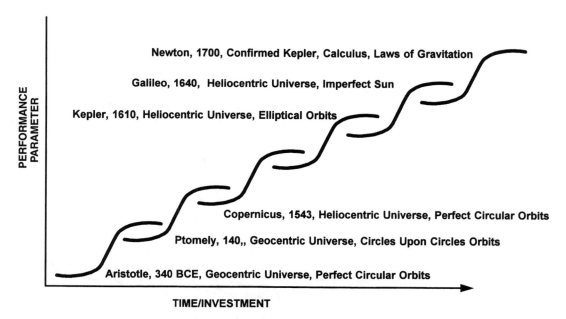

Figure 8.1   Classical physics "S" curve thinking on celestial motion. The classical understanding of celestial motion went through a series of insights that can be represented as "S" curves.

applied to any other subject of consequence. It is the most important discipline of business. Every cockamamie idea that is offered is not of equal value. Much of what is routinely reported and quoted in the I/T media is not good or bad strategy; it is nonstrategy completely devoid of any strategic thinking content.

The Art of War provides an enduring basis for building a winning strategy that transcends changing times and varied circumstances. I believe that corporate leadership should be given an annual written and oral test on *The Art of War* and, if they fail, should be removed. Sun Tzu said

> The lives of the people and the order of the nation are in the charge of the generals. When their assistance is complete, the country is strong. When their assistance is defective, the country is weak.

Is strategic thinking and the development of a deep and far-reaching strategy not the supreme responsibility of the executive leadership. If they are not to be Sunian strategists, what are they to be?

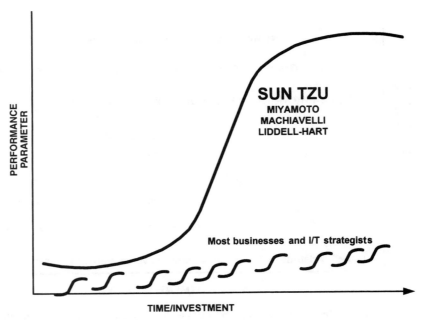

Figure 8.2 Stategic thinking "S" curve. Sun Tzu's cognitive strategy "S" curve continues unchallenged.

It has been suggested that the "S" curve concept (see Chapter 3) which is used to model the life cycle productivity of technologies can be used equally well to model the life cycle efficacy of ideas. Figure 8.1 illustrates the use of "S" curves to model the substitution and diffusion of the understanding of the laws of celestial motion from Aristotle to Newton.[1] Each idea was eventually replaced by a better theory as it was unable to accurately explain reality. Figure 8.2 illustrates a strategy "S" curve for the strategic thinking of Sun Tzu. It is my estimation that most modern strategic thinkers don't even come close to displacing it. Who you chose as your strategy teacher is extremely important. It defines your grand view of problems. You can do much worse than choosing the greater master, but it is highly argumentative whether you can do better.

This completes the question and answer period. As I said, nobody was shy, but I actually relish the joust. It is the excitement of competing ideas that keeps my job fun and always fresh. I'd be happy to hear your ideas as well. Please reach me on the internet at bernie.boar@newbrunswicknj.attgis.com.

9

Vision Is Seeing Victory Before It Exists

As is common with most people who are captivated by the discipline of strategy, I find the subject of leadership to be most fascinating. Why are some people leaders? How do leaders lead? Why do others follow? Are leaders born or made or both? The questions are incredibly important, but they are not comfortably answered.

In spite of my investigative efforts, I was never satisfied with the answers I uncovered until I read *The Art of War.* Sun Tzu said

> Vision [leadership] is seeing victory before it exists. This is the strategist [leader's] way to strategic triumph.

These 15 words encapsulate the essence of leadership. A leader sees future success when it is still unknowable and beyond comprehension by most, and galvanizes the organization to achieve that future.

Sun Tzu's idea of leadership is far more powerful then competing conventional ideas. Most modern strategy theorists suggest that the leader-strategist should have a distinct point of view about the future, should set a direction for the organization, or should anticipate discontinuities.[1] For a Sunian leader, this is woefully inadequate. A Sunian leader must not only have a point of view about the future, he must foresee how he will win in that future and how he will make that future materialize out of its current formlessness. So a Sunian leader sees what others do not see and knows what others do not know.

When I work with clients in developing a strategy, at the final session I ask if they are excited about what they have prepared. Without forewarning, I ask the most senior executive to come to the front of the room to recount for us the story of our future victory. If "vision [leadership] is seeing victory before it exists," then it is the responsibility of the leadership, before empowering the organization with strategy execution, to narrate the history of the future triumph. After a moment of surprise, most people quickly compose themselves, reflect, and let their imagination take command. The recounting of our future victory is a most moving moment for the team, and we end the strategy preparation on an emotional high.

As the author of this book, it is my responsibility to recount the history of our future triumph. Our victory occurred as follows:

> While we were excited and energized, we were not so innocent as to believe that there was not a lot of skepticism and cynicism about our intent. Many openly said that they thought our plan to migrate to C/S was simply today's *strategic programme du jour.* After the initial hoopla settled, everything would return to normal as it always had before.
>
> We, however, had a shared vision of a very different I/T: an I/T that could be used as a strategic weapon to create opportunities of growth for the business. We built our strategy on five simple ideas:
>
> 1. Massive reeducation of and communication to our people.
> 2. Architecture would be the linchpin of all our actions.
> 3. Pathfinder projects would find the way.
> 4. We would start small, gain acceptance, and evolve.
> 5. We would build and sustain commitment because commitment generates belief and belief generates the most valuable asset of all—extended and Herculean *effort* against the friction to change.
>
> Though our vision was deep and far-reaching, our implementation would be pragmatic and incremental. We really had no other choice. Even if we had had perfect technology and unanimous support, we didn't have the resources to keep what was running and rebuild everything anew overnight.
>
> After we developed our unifying reach, range, and maneuverability architecture, we started with three families of applications. In this way, we could test the economies of sharing cost theory. One family was a set of decision support systems, one was a family of information exchange systems, and the last was an important but not mission critical family of transaction systems. All had extensive sharing opportunities, and operational flexibility was of prime business importance.
>
> Things started slowly, certainly much more slowly then we had hoped for, but there was a large learning curve. New tech-

nologies had to be installed, new competencies developed, new processes built, and new relationships created. We had to learn, and learn we did. It was all *new*.

Slowly at first, and then ever faster, we started to see remarkable progress. The users loved that we used an iterative prototyping methodology to gather requirements. The operations organizations committed to change and threw themselves into developing new OA&M procedures. Our training organization was great in how it contracted and developed new courses.

As the system went on-line, we crossed our fingers. It was successful beyond our wildest hopes. It was successful not because of what we had built but because of our new-found flexibility. The users had been sold flexibility, and they quickly tested us. We responded in kind, and I remember my peer in the user organization buying pizza and sodas for the developers for the first time after the developers made a crucial change that he never believed they could do in a week. We saw our vision unfold before our eyes.

Success is the best prescription for pessimism, and quickly the rest of the organization jumped in. It is now 6 years later, and we just unplugged our last mainframe. I believe that a savings of 30 to 40 % would be a reasonable estimate. It was not easy, it was not without setbacks, but it works as our vision imagined it. We offer not only more efficient I/T, we offer incredibly malleable I/T. We are not only an I/T success, we are, more important, a success for the business. We are now included in all business strategy sessions and are asked to give briefings on how I/T may be used to radically alter the business. More then anything else, our migration transformed us from being viewed as an expense to be ruthlessly cut to being seen as a cherished weapon of business advantage. Our triumph is complete.

So we now come to work every day as respected and trusted business partners. Our I/T systems let our business fight a war of maneuver, and we are winning. We attack the marketplace like a swarm of bees. We have overlaid incredible I/T flexibility upon our environmental business diversity (Figure 9.1). But I am concerned that we do not rest on our laurels. We will start next week implementing our next radical vision of our I/T organization. We must continue to innovate. We must endlessly continue to innovate because *they will come*.

The bitter and hard truth is that mainframe computing never had a chance of becoming strategic computing. The emotional and political attachments to the mainframe are readily understandable,

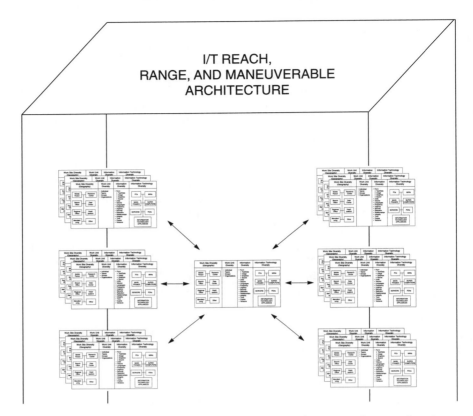

Figure 9.1   **I/T flexibility. The primal strategic reason for moving to CSC is to be able to economically overlay the business environment diversity with inexhaustible computing adaptability.**

but the logic of strategy and the market do not care. Host-centered computing never had a chance because it lacked the most important quality of strategic computing—*limitless adaptability.*

Sun Tzu said

> Victory is not repeated but adopts its form endlessly. The ability to gain victory by adapting to an opponent is called genius. *Adaptive maneuver must be limitless.*

Strategic computing requires computing assets that are formless, inscrutable, and unfathomable, and whose adaptability is inexhaustible. When your computing capability is such, against what do your opponents attack, against what do your opponents defend? Mainframe computing never had a chance.

Our MPS associates asked, "Why are we moving off the mainframe?" We are moving off the mainframe because in the next millennium I/T must be used as a weapon of strategic advantage, and the attributes of advantage belong to client/server computing, not mainframe computing. Client/server computing will be the first form of I/T that earns the designation of being a *strategic configuration of power*.

A strategic configuration of computing powerful enough to respond to the needs of the knowledge age (Figure 9.2)[2] where information is the basis of knowledge and knowledge is the basis of wealth. That is why we are moving to CSC. Our refutation is now complete.

NOTES

1. For example, one well-known contemporary strategy authority said, "Industry foresight is what top managers really compete for—to develop the best point of view of the future."

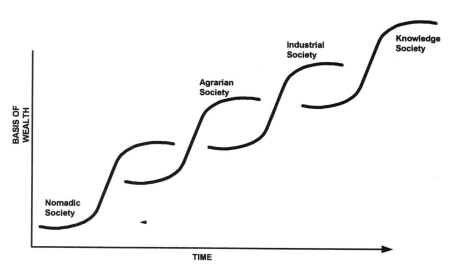

Figure 9.2   The basis of wealth. In the twenty-first century, information and knowledge will become the basis of wealth.

2. Figure 9.2 uses the "S" curve concept to illustrate the changes that have occurred in the basis of economic wealth over the centuries. These shifts can be understood as follows:

- *Nomadic Society:* The symbol of the era was the hunting club and the basis of wealth was the excellence of the hunters. If you had capable hunters, you ate else you starved.
- *Agrarian Society:* The symbol of the era was the plow and the basis of wealth was fertile land. Whoever owned the land and could grow adequate food stores was wealthy.
- *Industrial Society:* The symbol of the era was the gasoline engine and the basis of wealth was land, labor and capital. This is the era that we were born into but it is coming to an end.
- *Knowledge Society:* The symbol of this emerging era is the chip. Wealth will be a function of whoever can best collect, disseminate, and analyze information to create value.

In the Knowledge Society, your information assets are no longer an unfortunate but necessary expense, they are the means of creating economic value.

Appendix A
The Mainframe Preservation Society Bibliography

1. "An Easy Seduction," *Computing,* February 1994.
2. "Do Client/Server and OLTP Mix?" *Network Computing,* 2/15/94.
3. "United We Stand, Client/Server We Fall," *Datamation,* 2/1/94.
4. "Pitfalls of Client/Server Computing," *DBMS,* August 1993.
5. "Use C/S for Benefits, Not to Save Money," *Network World.*
6. "Benefits, Not Buzzwords," *Software Magazine,* 1/6/94.
7. "Open Systems, A Bad Idea," *Computerworld,* 4/19/93.
8. "The Client/Server Challenge," *Harvard Business Review,* July/August 1994.
9. "Mainframe Comeback," *Forbes ASAP.*
10. "Return of the Dinosaurs," *Business Week.*
11. "So How Much Does It Cost?" *PC Week,* 7/11/94.
12. "The Great Unseen Cost of Client/Server," *PC Week,* 7/11/94.
13. "Client/Server Costs, Don't Get Taken for a Ride," *Datamation.*
14. "Unsupportable Costs," *Open Computing,* February 1994.
15. "Client/Server Costs More Than Expected," *Computerworld.*
16. "Downsizing Costs Concern Client/Server Users," *Infoworld.*
17. "The Downside of Downsizing," *Networking Management,* December 1992.
18. *The Dinosaur Myth,* Xephon Consulting.
19. "The Perils of Peer Pressure," *Information Week,* 3/21/94.
20. "Fighting the High Costs of Client/Server Computing," *Data Communications,* 5/21/94.
21. "Dispelling Mainframe Myths," *Datamation,* 5/15/94.
22. "Downsizing Costs Concern C/S Users," *Infoworld,* 12/13/93.
23. "Big Iron Isn't Dead," *GCN,* 7/19/93.
24. "Enterprise Client/Server Costs," *Unix Review,* January 1994.

25. "A Guide For Estimating C/S Costs," *GARTNER Group*, 4/18/94.

26. "Chaos of the Desktop," *DBMS*, July 1994.

27. "Quote of the Week," *Information Week*, 10/25/93.

28. "Junk My Mainframe?" *Computerworld*, 5/31/94.

29. "Large Shops Rethink PC Focus," *Computerworld*, 2/14/94.

30. "Deployment Data," *PC Week*, 7/4/94.

31. "Don't Be So Quick to Rip the Mainframe," *Computerworld*, 11/29/93.

32. "Facing the C/S Locomotive," *SMS Research Note*, 4/5/93.

33. "Exploring Downsizing's Hidden Costs," *Software Magazine*, March 1993.

34. "What Do Mainframes Cost?" *Enterprise Systems Journal*, July 1994.

35. "Preparing for the Hidden Costs of Client/Server," *Client/Server Today*, January 1995.

36. "Cost of Computing: A Comparative Study of Mainframe and PC/LAN Installations," *ITG*.

Appendix B

The Proprietary Systems Conservation Society Bibliography

1. "Open Systems, a Bad Idea," *Computerworld*, 4/19/93.
2. *The Dinosaur Myth*, Xephon Consulting.
3. "Don't Get Locked in the Open," *PC Magazine*, 3/29/94.
4. "Look Before You Leap to the Promised Land of Open Systems," *Digital News*.
5. "Argumentum Proprietarius," *DEC Professional*.
6. "The Standard Excuses," *HP Professional*.
7. "Is Being Half Open Like Being Half Pregnant?" *Computerworld*, 12/6/93.
8. "The Open Systems Paradox," *DBMS*, June 1994.

Appendix C
Data Architecture Bibliography

1. Adams, "OLTP," *Federal Computer Week,* 5/18/92.
2. Asbeck, "The Partitioned Multi-Objective Risk Method," *Large Scale Systems* 6, 1984.
3. Atre, *Distributed Databases, Cooperative Processing and Networking,* McGraw-Hill, 1992.
4. Bloor, "Postponing A Dream," *DBMS,* October 1993.
5. Boar, *Implementing Client/Server Computing: A Strategic Perspective,* McGraw-Hill, 1993.
6. Bright, A. Hurson, and S. Pakzad, "A Taxonomy of Current Issues in Multidatabase Systems," *Computer,* March 1992.
7. Burleson, "Managing Distributed Databases," *Database Programming and Design,* June 1994.
8. Caberra, J. McPheason, P. Schwartz, and J. Wyllie, "Implementing Atomicity in Two Systems," *IEEE Transactions on Software Engineering,* Vol. 19, No. 19, October 1993.
9. Chorafas, *Handbook of Database Design and Distributed Relational Databases,* Tab Books, 1989.
11. Ciciani, D. Dias, and P. Yu, "Analysis of Concurrency-Coherency Control," *IEEE Transactions of Software Engineering,* Vol. 19, No. 10, October 1992.
12. Comaford, "TP Monitors Enable Database Flexibility," *PC Week,* 4/4/94.
13. "Data Replication Heats Up," *Distributed Computing Monitor,* Vol. 8 No. 11.
14. Dolgicer, "The Acid Test for Distributed Transactions," *Data Communications,* June 1993.
15. Elmagarmid (editor), *Database Transaction Models for Advanced Applications,* Morgan Kaufmann, 1993.
16. Engler, "The Dollars Are in the Detail," *Open Computing,* October 1994.

17. Gallagher, "Replication Eases Data Distribution," *PC Week,* 11/30/92.
18. Gray, *Transaction Processing,* Morgan Kaufmann, 1993.
19. Haimes, "Total Risk Management," *Risk Analysis,* Vol. 11, No. 2, 1991.
20. Hansen and J. Hansen, *Database Management and Design,* Prentice Hall, 1992.
21. Kaplan, "On the Quantitative Definition of Risk," *Risk Analysis* 1, 1981.
22. Korzeniowski, "More Features Overlapping Between DBMS, OLTP Monitors" *Software Magazine,* September 1992.
23. Loosley, "Learning from Experience," *Database Programming and Design,* October 1993.
24. Loosley, "A Three Tier Solution," *Database Programming and Design,* February 1994.
25. Quinlan, "Heterogeneous Distributed Databases," *Database Programming and Design,* October 1993.
26. Martin, *Design and Strategy for Distributed Data Processing,* Prentice Hall, 1981.
27. McClarn, *OLTP Handbook,* McGraw-Hill, 1993.
28. McGoveran, "Two-Phased Commit or Replication," *Database Programming and Design,* May 1993.
29. Ozsu and P. Valduriez, "Distributed Database Systems: Where Are We Now?" *Database Programming and Design,* March 1992.
30. Richter, "Distributing Data," *Byte,* June 1994.
31. Schussel, "Database Replication: Watch the Data Fly," *Client/Server Today,* October 1994.
32. Statler, "Transaction Monitor technology," *DEC User,* August 1992.
33. The, "Distributed Data Without Choking the Net," *Datamation,* January 1994.
34. VanName and B. Catchings, "Two-Phased Commit," *PC Week,* 5/30/94.
35. White, "Let the Replication Battles Begin," *Database Programming and Design,* May 1994.

Appendix D

The Art of War *Bibliography*

TRANSLATIONS OF *THE ART OF WAR*

1. *The Art of War,* Sun Tzu, Translated by Thomas Cleary, Shambhala Dragon Editions, 1988.
2. *The Art of War,* Sun Tzu, Translated by Samuel B. Griffith, Oxford University Press, 1963.
3. *The Art of War,* Sun Tzu, Translated by L. Giles, Luzac & Co, 1910.
4. *The Art of Strategy,* Sun Tzu, Translated by R. L. Wing, Dolphin Press, 1988.
5. *The Seven Military Classics of Ancient China Including The Art of Strategy,* Sun Tzu, Translated by R. D. Sawyer, Westview, 1993.

ARTICLES AND BOOKS ABOUT *THE ART OF WAR*

- "For White Collar Warriors," Sherry, Andrew, *Far Eastern Economic Review,* July 21, 1994.
- "Strategic Management Thought in East Asia," Tung, Rosalie L., *Organizational Dynamics,* Spring 1994.
- "Sun Tzu's Strategic Thinking and Contemporary Business," Chen, Min., *Business Horizons,* March/April 1994.
- "Sun Tzu's Art of Stock-Picking," Lucas, Louise, *Asian Business,* March 1994.
- "Honda and The Art of Competitive Manoeuvre," Benjamin, Chris, *Long Range Planning,* August 1993.

- *"The Art of War* and the Art of Management," Floyd, Raymond E., *Industrial Management,* September/October 1992.
- "The Gospel According to Sun Tzu," Romm, Joseph J., *Forbes,* December 9, 1991.
- "Adjusting to the Job of Strategist: Tactical Advice from an Old Soldier," Cloud, Avery, *Computerworld,* July 23, 1990.
- *The Asian Mind Game,* Chin-Ming, Chu, Rawson Associates, 1991.

Appendix E
Technology Substitution and Diffusion Bibliography

1. F. Bass, V. Mahajan, and E. Muller, "New Product Diffusion Models in Marketing," *Journal of Marketing*, Vol. 54, January 1990.
2. F. Bass and J. Norton, "A Diffusion Theory Model of Adoption and Substitution for Successive Generations of High Technology Products," *Management Science*, Vol. 33, No. 9, September 1987.
3. F. Bass and J. Norton, "Evolution of Technological Generations," *Sloan Management Review*, Winter 1992.
4. J. Fisher and R. Pry, "A Simple Substitution Model of Technological Change," *Technological Forecasting and Social Change*," Vol. 3, 1971.
5. R. Foster, "The Attacker's Advantage," *Summit Books*, 1986.
6. U. Kumar and V. Kumar, "Technological Innovation Diffusion," *IEEE Transactions on Engineering Management*, Vol. 39, No. 2, May 1992.
7. H. Linestone and D. Sahal, "Technological Substitution," *Elsevier*, 1976.
8. C. Smith, "Responding to Substitution Threats," *Journal of Engineering and Technology Management*, Vol. 7, 1990.
9. C. Smith, "Understanding Technological Substitution," *Journal of Engineering and Technology Management*, Vol. 9, 1992.

Index

229